FACE THE ISSUES

Intermediate Listening
and
Critical Thinking Skills

CAROL NUMRICH

in cooperation with

National Public Radio

Longman

New York & London

Face the Issues: Intermediate Listening and Critical Thinking Skills

Longman, 10 Bank Street, White Plains, N.Y. 10606

Associated companies:
Longman Group Ltd., London
Longman Cheshire Pty., Melbourne
Longman Paul Pty., Auckland
Copp Clark Pitman, Toronto

NPR and Longman have tried unsuccessfully to locate the copyright owners of the introductory
background music used on the cassette for Unit 3. It is therefore included without permission or
credit. Longman accepts responsibility and welcomes any information as to its source.

The profiles in Unit 3 were adapted from *New York* magazine, December 21, 1981.

Acknowledgments and credits can be found on pages 153 and 154.

Distributed in the United Kingdom by Longman Group
Ltd., Longman House, Burnt Mill, Harlow, Essex CM20
2JE, England, and by associated companies, branches,
and representatives throughout the world.

Executive editor: Joanne Dresner
Development editor: Penny Laporte
Production editor: Linda Carbone
Text design: Helen L. Granger, Levavi & Levavi, Inc.
Cover design: Joseph DePinho
Text art: Robin Hessel Hoffmann
Photo research: Elizabeth Barker, Polli Heyden
Production supervisor: Priscilla Taguer

Library of Congress Cataloging-in-Publication Data

Numrich, Carol.
    Face the issues : intermediate listening and critical thinking
  skills / by Carol Numrich, in cooperation with National Public
  Radio.
        p.   cm.
    ISBN 0-8013-0300-1
    1. English language—Textbooks for foreign speakers.   2. Critical
  thinking.   3. Listening.   I. National Public Radio (U.S.)
  II. Title.
  PE1128.N84   1990
  428.3'4—dc20   89-8160
                                                          CIP

9 10-AL-959493

CONTENTS

INTRODUCTION

Face the Issues: Intermediate Listening and Critical Thinking Skills consists of twelve authentic radio interviews and reports from National Public Radio. The broadcasts were taken from "All Things Considered," "Morning Edition," and "Weekend Edition–Sunday."

Designed for intermediate students of English as a Second Language, the text presents an integrated approach to developing listening comprehension and critical thinking skills. By using material produced for the native speaker, the listening selections provide content which is interesting, relevant, and educational. At the same time, they expose the non-native speaker to unedited language, including the hesitations, redundancies, and various dialectical patterns which occur in everyday speech.

Each unit presents either a dialog or discussion of an issue of international appeal. The students gain an understanding of American values and culture as they develop their listening skills. Throughout each unit, students are encouraged to use the language and concepts presented in the listening material and to reevaluate their point of view.

SUGGESTIONS FOR USE

The exercises are designed to stimulate an interest in the material by drawing on students' previous knowledge and opinions and by aiding comprehension through vocabulary and guided listening exercises. In a variety of discussion activities, the students finally integrate new information with previously held opinions.

1 Predicting

In this exercise, students are asked to read the title of the interview or report and predict the content of the unit. This exercise should take a very short time— two or three minutes.

Some of the titles require an understanding of vocabulary or idiomatic expressions which the teacher may want to explain to the students. The ideas generated by the students can be written on the blackboard. Once the students have listened to the interview or report, they can verify their predictions.

2 Think Ahead

Before listening to the tape, students are asked to discuss the issues to be presented in the interview or report. In groups of four or five, the students discuss their answers to general questions or react to statements which include ideas from the broadcast. The students draw on their own knowledge or experience for this activity. It is likely that students will have different opinions and the discussion, especially with a verbal class, could become quite lengthy. It is recommended that the teacher limit this discussion to ten or fifteen minutes, so as not to exhaust the subject prior to the listening activities.

3 Vocabulary

In this section, three types of exercises are presented to prepare the students for vocabulary and expressions used in the listening selection.

Vocabulary in a reading text. In these exercises, vocabulary is presented in a reading passage which also introduces some of the ideas from the broadcast. The students should read through the text once for global comprehension. Then, as they reread the text, they match the vocabulary items with synonyms or short definitions. The meaning of the new words may be derived from context clues, from general knowledge of the language, or from a dictionary.

Vocabulary in sentences. In these exercises, vocabulary is presented in sentences which relate to the ideas in the listening selection. Context clues are provided in each sentence. The students should first try to guess the meaning of these words by supplying their own definition or another word which they think has similar meaning. Although the students may not be sure of the exact meaning, they should be encouraged to guess. Research suggests that this will lead them to a better understanding of the new words. Once they have tried to determine the meaning of these words through context, they match the words with definitions or synonyms.

Vocabulary in word groups. These exercises focus on the relationship between specific vocabulary items from the listening selection and other words. A set of three words follows a given vocabulary item; in each set, two words have similar meaning to the vocabulary item. It is suggested that the students work together to discuss what they know about these words. Through these discussions, they will begin to recognize roots and prefixes, and how these words relate to each other. The students should be encouraged to use a dictionary for this exercise.

4 Task Listening

This exercise presents the students with a global comprehension task before asking them to focus on more specific information in the listening selection. The "task" is purposely simple to help students focus on an important point in the recorded material. Consequently, most of the students should be able to answer the questions after the first listening.

5 Listening for Main Ideas

The second time students hear the recorded material, they are given questions to guide them in comprehending the main ideas of the listening selection. Each interview or report has between three and five main ideas which have been used to divide the selection into Parts. Each Part is introduced by a beep on the tape. The students are asked to choose the answers which best express the main ideas. The teacher should stop the tape at the sound of the beep to make sure the students have chosen an answer. The students may then compare their answers to see whether they agree on the main ideas. Only one listening is usually required for this exercise; however, some classes may need to listen twice in order to agree on the main ideas.

6 Listening for Details

In the third listening, the students are asked to focus on detailed information. The students are first asked to read either true and false statements or multiple choice questions. The teacher should clarify any items which the students do not understand. Then each Part of the recording is played. The students choose the correct answers as they listen, thus evaluating their comprehension. Finally, in pairs, they compare answers. The teacher should encourage the students to defend their answers based on their comprehension. They should also be encouraged to use the language from the tape to convince the other students of the accuracy of their answers. There will certainly be disagreements over some of the answers; the discussions will help focus attention on the information needed to answer the questions correctly. By listening to each Part another time, the students generally recognize this information. Once again, they should be asked to agree on their answers. If there are still misunderstandings, the tape should be played a third time, with the teacher verifying the answers and pointing out where the information is heard on the tape. It is important to note that some of the questions require interpretation or inference.

7 Looking at Language

In this exercise, an interesting point of language from the recorded material is presented in isolation, as a further aid to comprehension. In each broadcast, the use of grammar, idioms, or language is highlighted. The students are asked to listen to a segment from the listening selection and to focus on this use of language in context. Then, through discussions and exercises, the students practice the language in a different context. These exercises are not meant to be exhaustive, but rather to point out an interesting use of language. The teacher may want to supplement this exercise.

8 Follow-up Activities

In this section, three activities are presented. The teacher may want to choose only one, or perhaps choose one oral and one writing activity. The students should be encouraged to incorporate in their writing and discussions the vocabulary and concepts that were presented in the interview or report. It is expected that the students will synthesize the information gathered from the broadcast with their own opinions.

Discussion questions. In groups, the students discuss their answers to one or more of the questions. Students will most likely have different points of view, and it is during this discussion that they are given the opportunity to present their views to each other.

Essay topics. These topics give the students the opportunity to react in writing to the interview or report.

Interactive processing activities. These final activities consist of surveys, debates, design activities, role-plays, and values clarification exercises, in which the students must solve problems or develop ideas that recycle the language and concepts in the interviews and reports. During these activities, the students will have an opportunity to creatively examine their beliefs about the issues presented.

THE LAST INNOCENT MEAL

1 PREDICTING

From the title, discuss what you think the interview is about.

THINK AHEAD

Hw for 4/17

In groups, discuss your answers to the following questions.

1. Do you eat breakfast every day? What is a typical breakfast in your country?
2. Do people in your country ever combine breakfast and lunch into a Sunday brunch? Which do you prefer, to have brunch, or to eat two separate meals? Why?
3. Who cooks your meals? Do you like to cook? If so, what do you cook best?

 VOCABULARY

Hw for 4/17

The following words will help you understand the interview. Try to guess the meaning of the words. Use your knowledge of English, or use your dictionaries. In each set of words, cross out the word that does not have a similar meaning to the italicized word. Then compare your answers with those of another student. Discuss why these words are similar. The first one has been done for you.

1. *trendy*	chic	stylish	~~old-fashioned~~
2. *overlooked*	disregarded	neglected	focused
3. *festive*	happy	gay	depressing
4. *ingredients*	mixtures	elements	parts
5. *gourmet shops*	specialty shops	delicacy shops	supermarkets
6. *oatmeal*	cereal	fruit	grain
7. *translucent*	clear	solid	see-through
8. *transform*	remain	change	alter
9. *accustomed to*	used to	attracted to	familiar with
10. *lumpy*	with pieces	smooth	rough
11. *soupy*	thick	watery	thin

read rest of ch. for 4/17

4 TASK LISTENING

Listen to the interview. Find the answer to the following question.

| What is the example of good breakfast food? | *oatmeal* |

5 LISTENING FOR MAIN IDEAS

Listen to the interview again. The interview has been divided into three parts. You will hear a beep at the end of each part. As you listen, circle the answer that best expresses the main idea in that part. Compare your answers with those of another student.

PART 1 Why has Marian Cunningham written *The Breakfast Book*?

    a. She thinks people have stopped eating breakfast.

    b. She thinks breakfast has been overlooked.

    c. She wanted to share her gourmet recipes.

PART 2 How would you describe her recipe for oatmeal?

    a. It's very complicated.

    b. You need a lot of ingredients.

    c. It's simple and basic.

PART 3 What's the best kind of oatmeal?

    a. Oatmeal which is lumpy and soupy

    b. Oatmeal made with rolled oats

    c. Oatmeal cake

6 LISTENING FOR DETAILS

Read the statements for Part 1. Then listen to Part 1 again and decide whether the statements are true or false. As you listen, write a *T* or *F* next to each statement. Compare your answers with those of another student. If you disagree, listen to Part 1 again.

PART 1

T _____ 1. Marian Cunningham is a newspaper columnist.

F _____ 2. Her book, *The Breakfast Book*, was published last year.

F _____ 3. She believes that breakfast is trendy and chic.

F _____ 4. She thinks that breakfast and brunch are similar.

T _____ 5. People often drink wine with brunch.

T _____ 6. In her opinion, breakfast food uses basic ingredients.

F _____ 7. To find good breakfast food ingredients, Marian Cunningham suggests going to gourmet shops.

Repeat the same procedure for Parts 2 and 3.

PART 2

T _____ 8. Marian Cunningham uses rolled oats in her recipe.

F _____ 9. You must use one cup of oats for the recipe.

F _____ 10. You have to add cold water and salt to the oats.

T _____ 11. The oatmeal stands overnight in the oven.

T _____ 12. In the morning, you reheat the oatmeal.

T _____ 13. The oatmeal is very translucent in the morning.

F _____ 14. With this recipe, the oatmeal doesn't taste like oats.

F _____ 15. You must cook the oatmeal the night before in a very hot oven.

PART 3

_____ 16. At summer camp, people laughed at the oatmeal.

_____ 17. The interviewer thinks oatmeal looks awful.

_____ 18. If oatmeal is lumpy, it's because it's too soupy.

_____ 19. Rolled oats are lump-proof.

_____ 20. Marian Cunningham likes oatmeal with sugar and heavy cream.

_____ 21. She likes to eat oatmeal with pound cake.

7 LOOKING AT LANGUAGE Verbs Used in Cooking

Exercise 1

In this interview, Marian Cunningham describes a recipe for "good, simple breakfast food." Listen to her description again and fill in the missing verbs.

Interviewer:

Give us an example of just plain, simple, good breakfast food.

Cunningham:

Well, I think that this would be a wonderful surprise to lots of people . . . the use of rolled oats. And this comes really from Scotland and Ireland. It's called "Irish oatmeal" sometimes, although it is, these are rolled oats and not the steel-cut oats. But simply taking, let's say, a cup or maybe only ⅔ cup of oats

and ___pour___ 1½ cups of boiling water over it, with
1

a little salt in the water. ___stir___ it,
2

___cover___ it, and ___let___ it ___stand___
3   4

overnight, preferably in a very low oven, 200 degrees,

all night long. In the morning, I simply ___heat___
5

it as hot as I wish, and ___stir___ and ___serve___ .
6   7

Exercise 2

Work with another student. Look at the chart below. The verbs from Exercise 1 have been put into categories on the chart. Discuss the meaning of these verbs.

Combining Ingredients	Changing the Consistency of Food	Preparing to Cook	Cooking Food	Getting Ready to Eat
pour stir add beat combine mix blend measure sift cream	let stand sift cream beat	cover preheat grease	heat bake	serve

Now read the following recipe for pound cake. Discuss the meaning of the italicized verbs. Use your dictionaries to help you. Then write them on the chart in the appropriate category. Some words may be used in more than one category.

Pound Cake

Preparation time: 30 minutes
Cooking time: 1 hour

Ingredients

4 cups flour   3 cups sugar
1 tsp. salt   8 eggs
4 tsp. baking powder 1 cup milk
1 1/2 cups butter   2 tsp. vanilla

Directions

Preheat oven to 325°. *Sift* the flour before measuring. *Measure* 4 cups of flour and sift again with salt and baking powder.

Cream the butter until soft. *Add* the sugar and continue creaming. *Beat* the eggs in a separate bowl. *Combine* the eggs and sugar mixture. Combine the flour mixture with the milk and vanilla. *Mix* all the ingredients. *Blend* thoroughly.

Grease two 4 1/2 x 8-inch loaf pans. *Bake* for 1 hour.

Exercise 3

Recipes are generally written very simply. The directions are clear and to the point. A well-designed recipe usually gives:

1. The ingredients, in the order you need to use them;
2. The exact measurements for each ingredient;
3. The time for preparation and cooking;
4. The steps for preparing the ingredients and instructions on how to cook them.

Using some of the vocabulary from the chart and the design of the pound cake recipe, write one of your favorite recipes. *HW for 4/24*

8 FOLLOW-UP ACTIVITIES

Discussion Questions

In groups, discuss your answers to the following questions.

1. In your opinion, which is the most important meal of the day? Why?
2. How does your life-style influence the way you eat? Is it possible to eat simple, healthy food in today's busy world?

HW for 4/17

Essay Topics

Choose one of the following topics.

1. Do you agree with Marian Cunningham that breakfast is "the last innocent meal"? Write an essay in which you express your opinion.
2. Does eating have a festive/celebratory role in your life? Or, do you think people focus too much on eating when they are in social situations? Write an essay in which you express your opinion.

Design A Breakfast Menu

In this interview, Marian Cunningham spoke about oatmeal, a simple breakfast food. She wrote a book about breakfast because she felt it was a meal that was overlooked.

Work in groups. Read the following situation and design a breakfast menu.

THE SITUATION

You own a restaurant which specializes in Sunday brunches. When it first opened, your restaurant was very successful. However, over the past few years, many new restaurants have opened up in your neighborhood. They also specialize in brunch.

Last month you did a market survey. You asked people in the area about their eating habits. You discovered that more and more people are interested in eating good, simple breakfast food. Many of the people said they didn't always take the time to eat breakfast at home, but they would eat out if there were a restaurant that served breakfast on their way to work. Based on your survey, you have decided to change your brunch menu to a breakfast menu.

Look at the menu below. Redesign it so that you offer good, simple breakfast food. In planning, decide on the following:

- which foods and drinks you will continue to serve
- which foods and drinks you will no longer serve
- which foods and drinks you will add to the menu
- which prices you will change

Compare your menu with those of other groups.

SUNDAY BRUNCH
Served 11:30 P.M.–2:30 P.M.

EYE OPENERS
(Your choice of Bloody Mary, Mimosa, or a glass of champagne) $3.75

STARTERS
Soup of the Day $3.25
Fresh Fruit in Season $2.75

ENTREES
- Eggs Benedict
English muffin, Canadian bacon, and poached eggs topped with Hollandaise sauce $6.95

- Eggs Florentine
English muffin, freshly cooked spinach, and poached eggs topped with Hollandaise sauce $6.95

- French Toast
French bread dipped in egg batter, lightly browned, and sprinkled with cinnamon & powdered sugar . .$5.25
with fresh strawberries . . . .$ .75

ALL ITEMS ARE SERVED WITH ASSORTED
BREADS & MUFFINS, COFFEE OR TEA.

EXTRAS
Bacon $1.75
Sausage $1.75
Croissant $1.45

"The Last Innocent Meal" was first broadcast on *Morning Edition*, October 4, 1987. The interviewer is Susan Stamberg.

LIVING THROUGH DIVORCE

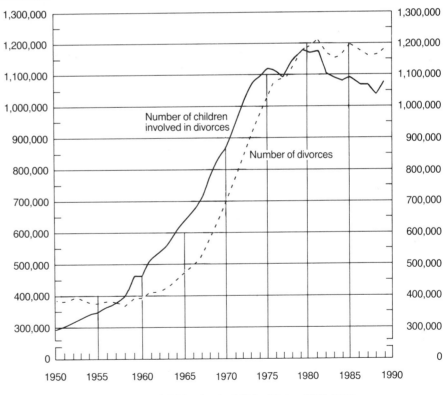

Divorces and children involved: United States, 1950–1989

1 PREDICTING

From the title, discuss what you think the interview is about.

Hw for 4/24 individually assigned

2 THINK AHEAD

In groups, discuss your answers to the following questions.

1. Look at the graph on page 9. How has the number of children involved in divorces in the U.S. changed since 1950?
2. Who suffers more in a divorce, parents or children?
3. Should parents who get divorced explain the reasons to their children?

Hw write for 4/24

3 VOCABULARY

The words in italics will help you understand the interview. Read the following sentences. Try to guess the meaning of these words from the context of the sentences. Then write a synonym or your own definition of the words.

1. Children often feel alone and don't know who they can *turn to* when their parents get divorced.

_____

2. It is difficult for children to *get used to* living with only one parent after their parents are divorced.

_____

3. People often find it difficult to explain their reasons for divorce. Is it the parents' responsibility to *share* these reasons with their children?

_____

4. When parents divorce they often have a difficult time *reassuring* their children and making them feel that everything will be all right.

_____

5. A child's first dance or music *recital* is a big event. Children feel it is important for their parents to attend.

_____

6. *Guidance counselors* work in schools to help children with their studies, but they sometimes help children with their family problems too.

7. Children suffer most when their parents first divorce; however, with time, they can usually *get through it.*

8. Perhaps the most difficult time for children is when they see one of their parents *packing up* to leave the home forever.

9. Children often think that their parents' divorce is their *fault;* they feel responsible for their parents' unhappiness.

10. Authors sometimes decide to write a *series* of books if their first book has been successful.

Now try to match the words and expressions with a definition or synonym. Then compare your answers with those of another student. The first one has been done for you.

b 1. turn to   a. performance

____ 2. get used to   b. ask for help

____ 3. share   c. responsibility for something bad

____ 4. reassure   d. a person who gives advice to students

____ 5. recital   e. prepare to leave

____ 6. guidance counselor   f. survive something

g. tell others about your experiences

____ 7. get through something   h. get into the habit of

____ 8. pack up   i. comfort

____ 9. fault   j. a continuing group of books or events

____ 10. series

4 TASK LISTENING

class 4/24 5/8   transcript opp. p. 134+

Listen to the interview. Find the answer to the following question.

Why is Betsy concerned about divorce? *her parents are getting divorced*

class 4/24 5/8

5 LISTENING FOR MAIN IDEAS

Listen to the interview again. The interview has been divided into three parts. You will hear a beep at the end of each part. As you listen, circle the answer that best expresses the main idea in that part. Compare your answers with those of another student.

PART 1 Why did Betsy Allison Walter write to Mayor Koch about her parents' divorce?

    a. She thought he was responsible for divorces in New York.
    b. She thought he was a good parent and would understand.
    (c.) She thought he knew a lot of things.

PART 2 How does Betsy feel about the advice that is given to her?

    a. She realizes that she is the only child with her problem.
    (b.) She still doesn't understand why her parents are getting divorced.
    c. She now understands why her parents can't stay together.

PART 3 What advice does Betsy give other children in her book?

    a. She tells them that it's their fault if their parents get divorced.
    b. She tells them not to cry.
    (c.) She says they should tell someone about their feelings.

class 4/24 5/8

6 LISTENING FOR DETAILS

Read the statements for Part 1. Then listen to Part 1 again and decide whether the statements are true or false. As you listen, write a *T* or *F* next to each statement. Compare your answers with those of another student. If you disagree, listen to Part 1 again.

PART 1

_F_ 1. Betsy Allison Walter is nine years old.

_T_ 2. Betsy lives in Manhattan.

_T_ 3. Betsy had no one to turn to.

_I_ 4. Betsy's father is with somebody else.

_I_ 5. Mayor Koch wrote back to Betsy.

_F_ 6. Mayor Koch gave her a solution to her problem.

_F_ 7. His letter was reassuring to Betsy.

_F_ 8. Betsy had hoped that the Mayor would call her father.

_F_ 9. Betsy's parents sat next to each other at her dance recital.

Repeat the same procedure for Parts 2 and 3.

PART 2

_F_ 10. Four hundred kids in Betsy's school have the same problem.

_T_ 11. The interviewer says most people have parents who are divorced.

_I_ 12. _The Boys' and Girls' Book of Divorce_ was written by a psychologist.

_F_ 13. Betsy went out to buy another book on divorce.

_F_ 14. She loved _The Boys' and Girls' Book of Divorce_.

_F_ 15. Betsy feels satisfied with people's answers about divorce.

_T_ 16. She thinks parents sometimes hide their reasons for divorce.

_T_ 17. Her father left the house.

_F_ 18. Betsy wants her parents to get divorced.

PART 3

_I_ 19. Betsy wrote a short book of advice.

_I_ 20. She reads the whole book in the interview.

_F_ 21. The interviewer gives Betsy advice about her parents.

_F_ 22. Betsy wants to be a writer and write a series of books.

_F_ 23. She would like to be rich.

_I_ 24. She would like to be famous.

class 5/8

7 LOOKING AT LANGUAGE Letter Writing

Exercise 1

There are seven basic parts to a letter. Read the following information about each part:

The date: In the United States, the date is written as: Month, Day, Year.

The sender's address: This is either printed on the top of the letter or typed on the top left side of the letter.

The salutation: This part opens the letter. It usually begins with "Dear . . ."

The body: This is the main part of the letter. It includes one or more paragraphs.

Special greeting: This can finish your message. It comes at the end of the body of the letter.

The close: This is the expression we use to finish the letter, before signing our name.

The signature: If the letter is typed, this is always written by hand, in ink. In formal letters the name is typed below the signature.

Now listen to Mayor Koch's letter to Betsy. As you listen, focus on the different parts of the letter. Then work with another student and label each of the seven parts.

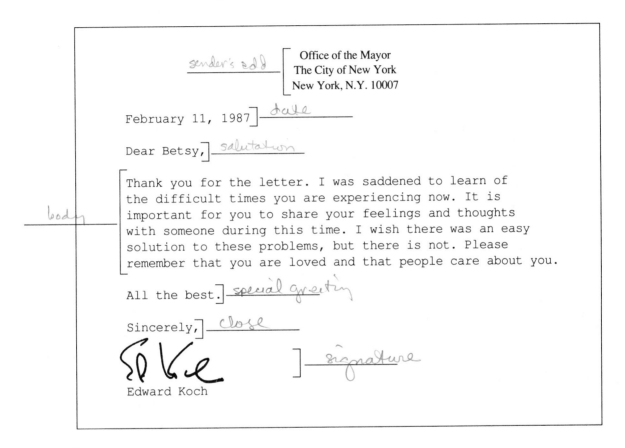

sender's add — Office of the Mayor
The City of New York
New York, N.Y. 10007

February 11, 1987 — date

Dear Betsy, — salutation

body —

Thank you for the letter. I was saddened to learn of the difficult times you are experiencing now. It is important for you to share your feelings and thoughts with someone during this time. I wish there was an easy solution to these problems, but there is not. Please remember that you are loved and that people care about you.

All the best. — special greeting

Sincerely, — close

— signature

Edward Koch

Exercise 2

1. The following variations can occur within the different parts of a letter. The choice of expression depends on the formality of the letter.

Work as a class. Discuss these different expressions. Decide if the expression should be used in formal or informal letters. Then write it in the chart below. Try to think of other examples and add them to the chart.

Salutation: Dear Eric,
Dear Mr. McCarthy:
Dear Sir:
To whom it may concern:

Special greeting at the end:	All the best. I look forward to hearing from you. Take care. Write soon.
The Close:	Love, Sincerely, Yours truly, Fondly,

Formal Expressions	Informal Expressions
Dear Mr. McCarthy :	*Dear Eric,*

2. Compare and contrast letter writing in your own countries to that in the United States. What expressions are used in opening and closing letters? In a letter, do you address people differently according to sex, profession, or relationship? How do you close a letter to different people in your country?

Exercise 3

Choose one of the following and write a letter.

1. Write your own letter to Betsy giving her advice on her problem.
2. Write a letter to Mayor Koch reacting to his advice to Betsy.

8 FOLLOW-UP ACTIVITIES

Discussion Questions

In groups, discuss your answers to the following questions.

1. Betsy wanted her parents to sit together during her dance recital, but they didn't. In your opinion, do divorced parents have an obligation to be together at important times in their child's life?
2. In Betsy's school, 75 percent of the children have parents who are divorced (300 out of 400). This percentage is not unusual in the United States. How does this percentage differ from the divorce rate in your country? What are the reasons for the difference or similarity?

Essay Topics

Choose one of the following topics.

1. Betsy's parents didn't explain their reasons for getting divorced to her. If you were Betsy's parents, would you discuss the reasons with her? Does it help children to accept their parents' divorce if they know the reasons for it? Write an essay in which you express your opinion.
2. Who is the best person to turn to when you experience pain: a friend, a parent, the school, the church? Write an essay in which you express your opinion and give your reasons.

disc. 5/8 HW-read → class discuss indiv. assigned

Case Studies The Question of Divorce

You have listened to a little girl express her feelings about her parents' divorce. You also have your own opinions on the issue of divorce.

Work in groups. Read each of the following cases. Then act as a group of family counselors. Discuss each case and agree on advice for each person. Take notes on your group's discussion. Then compare your suggestions with those of the other groups.

CASE 1: BETSY (AGE 8)

"My parents are getting divorced, and I really don't know who to turn to. My dad met another woman. I was just getting used to my life, and now this! It's really kind of hard on me. I invited both my parents to my dance recital, but they didn't sit next to each other. It was painful to see my dad packing up to leave. They won't explain anything to me."

CASE 2: GEORGE (AGE 66)

"My son has been married for ten years. His wife's a wonderful young woman. Over the years, my wife and I have grown quite attached to her. In fact, she's like a daughter to us. We've spent all the family holidays with them and we have even gone on vacations together. Now, after ten years, my son has decided to go off with another woman. He is divorcing his wife so that he can be with this new woman. We are very fond of our daughter-in-law, but don't know whether or not we should continue our relationship with her. Our son doesn't want us to continue seeing her."

CASE 3: CAROLYN (AGE 28)

"I married my husband five years ago. I was twenty-three years old . . . too young to know what I was doing. My life with him has become very boring. We never go out. We don't have any friends. I no longer want to be with him because we don't have anything in common. We have a two-year-old daughter, and I haven't wanted to think about getting a divorce. But I'm afraid that if my husband and I stay together, it will be even worse for her."

UNIT 2

CASE 4: JOHN (AGE 44)

"I have been seeing a married woman for six months now. She's been in a very unhappy marriage for years and is going to be getting a divorce soon. We've fallen in love and want to spend as much time together as possible. The problem is that she has a son. Every time I go over to her house I feel guilty because of her child. I know that he misses his father and doesn't appreciate me visiting his mother at the house. It's difficult for our relationship because we can't easily get together without her son. I don't know if I should continue this relationship until the divorce is final. In fact, I don't know if the relationship will ever work out because of her child and his relationship to his father."

CASE 5: JOYCE (AGE 50)

"I have been happily married for thirty years. This year my husband started acting differently towards me. He didn't seem to be interested in doing anything with me anymore. Finally I realized what had happened. He was seeing another woman. This other woman is half my age. She's twenty-five! I'm so depressed. I never thought that this could happen to me. My husband and I have discussed the matter; we've decided to get a divorce. My children are grown up and living on their own. I don't want to tell them about their father because I'm too ashamed."

"Living through Divorce" was first broadcast on *All Things Considered*, February 11, 1987. The interviewer is Noah Adams.

A BOY'S SHELTER FOR STREET PEOPLE

1 PREDICTING

From the title, discuss what you think the interview is about.

indiv assigned Hw for 5/15

2 THINK AHEAD

Work in groups. Read the following statements. Do you agree with them?
See if everyone in your group has the same opinion.

1. Society must help the people who have no homes and
   live on the street.
2. Most people who live on the street are there because
   they don't want to work.
3. You can usually tell what people are like by the way
   they look.
4. Most people who live on the street have mental
   problems.

Hw for 5/15   *read transcript for 5/15*

3 VOCABULARY

The following words will help you understand the interview. Try to guess
the meaning of the words. Use your knowledge of English, or use your
dictionaries. In each set of words, cross out the word that does not have
a similar meaning to the italicized word. Then compare your answers
with those of another student. Discuss why these words are similar. The
first one has been done for you.

1. *homeless*	street people	~~wealthy people~~	poor people
2. *startling*	amazing	calming	surprising
3. *resisted*	relented	opposed	fought
4. *impressionable*	affected by others	wise	easily influenced
5. *donation*	salary	gift	contribution
6. *volunteer*	help	charge	offer
7. *commitment*	comprehension	duty	obligation
8. *unconditionally*	politically	freely	without expectation
9. *threatening*	frightening	caring	scary
10. *campaign*	drive	religion	effort

transcript p. 137+

4 TASK LISTENING

Listen to the interview. Find the answer to the following question.

Who is interviewed with Trevor? *his father*

5 LISTENING FOR MAIN IDEAS

Listen to the interview again. The interview has been divided into four parts. You will hear a beep at the end of each part. As you listen, circle the answer that best expresses the main idea in that part. Compare your answers with those of another student.

PART 1 What did Trevor Ferrell do when he learned about the homeless?

   a. He asked his parents if he could live in the city.
   b. He asked the newspaper to write about the homeless.
   c. He tried to help the homeless.

PART 2 What did Trevor and his father learn about street life?

   a. They found out that the homeless do not want to work.
   b. They found out that living on the street is very hard.
   c. They found out that street life is not so bad.

PART 3 How does the community help the homeless?

   a. People bring them food in vans.
   b. The homeless stay with families.
   c. The community helps them find jobs.

PART 4 What has happened to Trevor because of his work with the homeless?

   a. He has more fun.
   b. His attitude has changed.
   c. He is more tired.

6 LISTENING FOR DETAILS

Read the questions for Part 1. Then listen to Part 1 again. As you listen, circle the best answer. Compare your answers with those of another student. If you disagree, listen to Part 1 again.

PART 1

1. When did Trevor first realize that people were living on the streets of Philadelphia?

   a. Two years ago

   b. In November

   c. Twelve months ago

2. How did Trevor learn about the homeless?

   a. From friends in the suburbs

   b. From his parents

   c. From a news report

3. How did Trevor's parents react when he wanted to go to the city to help someone?

   a. They were amazed.

   b. They thought it was a great idea.

   c. They were angry.

4. What did Trevor give to a man on the street?

   a. A blanket and pillow

   b. A note saying "God bless you"

   c. Food

5. What happened after Trevor's story was published?

   a. The local paper donated money.

   b. People volunteered to help.

   c. Trevor wrote a book.

Repeat the same procedure for Parts 2, 3, and 4.

PART 2

6. Which is *not* a name of Trevor's street friends?

    a. Chico

    b. Ralph

    c. Big Joel

7. What is *not* mentioned as a reason why people live on the street?

    a. They lost their jobs.

    b. They have mental problems.

    c. They are dirty.

8. How long did Trevor and his father stay on the street?

    a. A few minutes

    b. A few hours

    c. A few days

9. What happened when Trevor and his father tried to stay on the street?

    a. They were cold, so they went home.

    b. They were cold, but they slept in sleeping bags.

    c. They were cold because they slept on the sidewalk.

10. How did Trevor and his father feel about their night on the street?

    a. Proud

    b. Not proud

    c. Angry

11. What does Trevor's father think about the people living on the street?

    a. He thinks they're crazy.

    b. He doesn't think they have such a difficult life.

    c. He doesn't understand how they can live there.

PART 3

12. Who donates food to the homeless?

    a. Fast food chains

    b. Hospital coordinators

    c. The families of the homeless

13. Who pays for the food for the homeless?

    a. The homeless pay.

    b. No one pays.

    c. The city of Philadelphia pays.

14. What do the homeless need most?

    a. Caring

    b. Clothing

    c. Food

15. Why do people accept food from Trevor?

    a. Because he's a youngster

    b. Because he can help them to get a job

    c. Because he is threatening

PART 4

16. How has Trevor's life changed?

    a. He is not allowed to play with his friends as much.

    b. He is not able to play with his friends as much.

    c. He does not want to play with his friends as much.

17. How does Trevor feel about the change?

    a. It's worth it.

    b. He wishes he could help more.

    c. He is grateful for his new life.

18. What has Trevor learned from his experience?

   a. People are scary.

   b. People are nice.

   c. You should treat people according to the way they look.

19. How is the money from the book *Trevor's Place* used?

   a. His mother uses it for the family.

   b. It is used for Trevor's campaign.

   c. Trevor will use it for his college education.

7   LOOKING AT LANGUAGE   Passive Voice

Exercise 1

Listen again to Trevor's father describe how food is given to the homeless. Focus on the verbs in italics. Discuss who you think is doing these things.

> The vans go in every night serving homeless people food ... food that's generously *donated* by fast food chains ... and there are volunteer coordinators of the effort, individual families. There are over 100 families in the Philadelphia area that cook on a regular basis, and food *is taken in* and *given* freely, unconditionally, to people that are on the streets and obviously have a need for someone ... so much more of a need for the caring that's exchanged than really the food, I guess.

Explanation

In the three examples above, the focus is on the "food" rather than on the person or thing that does something with the food. We use the passive voice when we want to emphasize the "receiver" of the action rather than the person or thing that does the action. Trevor's father chose to focus on "food" rather than on the person or thing that was donating it, taking it in, or giving it away.

The passive voice, in any tense, is formed by the verb *to be* and the past participle. The person or thing that does the action is not always mentioned in the passive voice. When it is mentioned, it is introduced with the word "by". Notice the verb form and the use of "by" in each example:

Food *is* generously *donated by* fast food chains.
Food *is taken* in. (*by* volunteers)
Food *is given* freely. (*by* volunteers)

Exercise 2

Practice using the passive voice. Change the following sentences from active to passive voice. Be sure to use the same verb tense as in the original sentence. The first one has been done for you.

1. Fast food chains donate food to the homeless.

Food is donated to the homeless by fast food chains.

2. Volunteers give free food to the homeless.

Free food

3. Trevor helped the homeless.

4. A journalist interviewed Trevor.

5. Homeless people named the shelter "Trevor's Place."

Exercise 3

Read the following news story about Trevor's campaign for the homeless. Decide whether the focus is on the person or thing that does the action (active voice), or on the person or thing that receives the action (passive voice).

Complete the story with the verbs in parentheses. Use the active or passive voice in the simple past tense. The first two have been done for you.

New Shelter for City's Homeless

Many programs have recently been developed to help the city's homeless population. Perhaps the most interesting program is an eleven-year-old boy's campaign to help Philadelphia's homeless.

Two years ago, eleven-year-old Trevor Ferrell and his parents, Frank and Janet Ferrell, ___*put*___ (put) an ad
                                                                    1
in a local paper asking for donations to help Philadelphia's homeless. The paper was interested in finding out what Trevor and his parents were doing. Later that week, Trevor _*was interviewed*_ (interview) by the paper, and his story
        2
_____(publish). After the publication of that story,
        3
many people _____ (send) donations for the
                        4
homeless to Trevor and his family. Food _____
                                                5
(donate) by fast food chains. Many people_____
                                                        6
(volunteer) to help Trevor and his family. Someone even
_____(contribute) a van. Volunteers_____
        7   8
(start) to give out free food to people living on the streets.

But Trevor Ferrell's campaign did not stop there. Last week, a permanent shelter for the homeless_____
                                                                9
(open). Now many of Philadelphia's homeless have a

warm place to shower and sleep. Through his hard work,

Trevor has become friends with many of the homeless

people. The people know and love him. In fact, the shelter

_____ (name) "Trevor's Place" by the people who
     10

stay there.

8 FOLLOW-UP ACTIVITIES

Discussion Questions

In groups, discuss your answers to the following questions.

1. If you were Trevor's parents, would you support him in helping homeless people? Why or why not?
2. In your opinion, is it anyone's responsibility to take care of the homeless? If so, whose? Family members of the homeless? Volunteer families in the community? The city? The state? Others?

Essay Topics

Choose one of the following topics.

1. Trevor said that his experience with the homeless had changed his life completely. Have you ever had an experience that changed your life completely? Write an essay in which you discuss this experience.
2. Do you live in a city with homeless people? If so, write a letter to the mayor of your city. Describe the situation as you see it. Offer advice for solving the problem of people living on the streets.

Case Studies   Profiles of the Homeless

You have listened to some reasons why people live on the street. Now you will read some character profiles of homeless people in New York City. You will analyze the homeless situation based on these profiles.

Work in groups of five. Each person in the group will choose *one* of the profiles and prepare to give information about that person to the rest of the group. As you read, fill in the chart on page 33 with information from the profile. Then interview the others in your group. Use the chart to help you talk about the profile. Complete the rest of the chart as you listen to each others' descriptions.

After you fill in the information, use the chart to analyze and discuss the homeless situation. Follow the analyzing procedure on page 34.

DONALD

Donald has a neat appearance. He looks different from the rest of the men in the shelter where he stays. His eyes are clear; his appearance is neat; but, he looks frightened.

Donald is twenty-nine and represents a new type of homeless person. He is able to work, but has been forced onto the streets because he lost his job and can't find an apartment he can afford to rent.

A quiet, slender man, Donald worked for six years in a photography lab. When the company was sold to new owners, they fired more than half the employees. Since then, he has been trying to find work. He fills out application after application, but he can't get a job.

Four weeks ago, Donald lost his apartment. His unemployment money ran out. He has been on the streets ever since. He is trying to get welfare money, but he needs a permanent address where he can receive necessary documents. Without the documents, he cannot get welfare.

Donald comes from a religious family. He was taught to be kind to everyone, but he can't tolerate the life of the shelter; many of the people there are drug addicts and alcoholics. He can't sleep at night because he sees people taking drugs. He feels like he's going crazy.

Donald has no wife or children. His other relatives are living in the South. He doesn't want them to know how far he's fallen. He wants to get out of this situation. He's sure there is a better life for him somewhere.

FLORENCE

Florence, forty-three, a big, broad woman, wears an evening dress and a fake white fur coat. She is five months pregnant. She is not sure who the father of her baby is. She says that she'll know when the baby is born. She says she'll keep the baby if it's a girl. She has eight other children by three former husbands. Her last husband was over eighty years old.

Florence has been homeless for three years, on and off. She spent time in Los Angeles trying to be an actress, but she was not very successful. She also spent time in a mental institution seven or eight years ago.

Florence keeps her possessions in a locker in the downtown bus station. She spends her nights in the subways. She likes it in the subways because she can spend time with friends and talk about the Lord. She says she wants to marry the Lord.

JEAN

Jean, thirty-nine, spends sleepless nights walking around the neighborhood where she grew up. She enters buildings and looks through garbage to see if she can find clothes. Several years ago, she and her mother lost their home; the apartment building they lived in was burned down.

Jean was born mentally retarded. Yet, the way she speaks gives the impression of normal intelligence. Jean's mother was an alcoholic. She died of cancer about four years ago, and Jean has been homeless ever since.

Jean is a large woman. Her dark grey hair is freshly washed. It is important for her to stay clean. She doesn't want to smell like some of the other women in the subway. Jean often goes to a day shelter where she can get a shower and a meal.

Jean finishes her wandering every morning at 6:00 in a diner where the owner sometimes gives her two dollars. She tries to pay the owner back at the beginning of the month, when she receives her social security check.

GEORGE

George has white hair, a high forehead and angry eyes. Long ago, he taught physics at one of the city's major universities. Now he is very ill; his speech is unclear. He tells stories that don't make sense. He talks about "angels."

George appears to be in his early fifties. He carries all his things in a plastic shopping bag. His shirt is filthy. He is often infested with lice from sleeping on the streets.

However, a neighborhood church donated some clothes to George. He likes the people at the church and sometimes gets a free dinner there. People say that when he goes to the church he sometimes thinks clearly.

George spends many of his nights on a park bench. Sometimes he sits in an all-night cafe, when he has enough money for a few cups of coffee. When he hasn't eaten in awhile, the waiter in the cafe will usually give him something to eat on credit.

SALLY

Sally is a forty-five-year-old woman. She has one missing tooth and many clothes under her old dark coat, but otherwise she appears to be an ordinary, attractive woman. She is polite and her speech is clear. She carries a shopping bag full of books that she says she reads. In fact, she can intelligently discuss one of the books she is carrying. She says she identifies with some of the characters in the story.

Sally attended twelve years of school and an additional two years at a small-town community college. She has been living on the streets for only six weeks. She got divorced two years ago. Her ex-husband took most of the money after their divorce.

When Sally first came to New York, she lived in cheap hotels until she had no more money. Then she spent many nights in the waiting room of the downtown bus station. Finally she got a job with a food chain, but when she asked for a job transfer, she was fired.

She has two daughters: one is twenty years old, the other is twenty-two. The twenty-two-year-old has an apartment in the city. However, she and Sally don't get along very well, so Sally has decided to live on the street for now. Sometimes she sleeps in the bus station, where it's warm.

Sally tries to keep herself clean. She always carries clean clothes and a toothbrush with her. She takes a shower in one of the city's shelters whenever she can. She never thought she would end up in this situation.

	Age	Education	Job Experience	Present Housing Situation	Psychological Profile	Family Background
Donald						
Florence						
Jean						
George						
Sally						

Analyzing Procedure

1. Compare and contrast the information you have categorized on the chart. Can you find any similarities or differences?

2. Try to characterize the homeless population. Can you make generalizations about who these people are? Are there any characteristics that make it difficult to generalize?

3. Reevaluate your ideas or opinions about homeless people. Look at the statements on page 21, under *Think Ahead.* Do you have the same opinions about these statements as before? Discuss whether or not any of them have changed.

4. Analyze further. Find out more about the homeless. Where can you get further information?

"A Boy's Shelter for Street People" was first broadcast on *Morning Edition*, November 30, 1985. The interviewer is Lynn Neary.

WHERE THE GIRLS AND BOYS ARE

1 PREDICTING

From the title, discuss what you think the report is about.

2 THINK AHEAD

In groups, discuss your answers to the following questions.

1. In some areas of the United States there is a higher percentage of women than men. In other areas there is a higher percentage of men than women. Is this true in your country? If so, why?
2. Does employment influence where people live in your country? What kinds of jobs attract people to certain areas?

3 VOCABULARY

The words in italics will help you understand the report. Read the dialog. Try to determine the meaning of these words. Then match the words with their definitions or synonyms in the list at the end of the text. Write the number of each word next to its definition or synonym. Compare your answers with those of another student. The first one has been done for you.

Jane:

"It's really difficult to meet a man these days. There's an *abundance* of women working in my office, but only

two men, and they're both married! Even when I go out, it seems that there are so many women living in this city, but the men are as *rare* as fine wine. You

know, I can already imagine myself, years from now, an *elderly* person in this city, living alone and

unmarried!"

Interviewer:

"Well, you don't have to grow old without a man. If you're really so *longing* to meet someone, you might

have to move! You know, you're right about the number of women in this city. When you compare the number

of women and men here, there's an *overload* of women.
5

No wonder you can't find a partner, that perfect *mate*!"
6

Jane:

"I've heard that there are more women living in this town than men, but I wonder if it's really true. I mean, I wonder what the *statistics* would show."
7

Interviewer:

"Well, as a matter of fact, I just read a report the other day which said that men and women are not *spread evenly* across the United States. Some states
8

have more men, and others have more women. In fact, we're living in the city with the highest *concentration* of women in the country."
9

Jane:

"You're kidding! I'd like to read that report so I can see where the highest concentration of men is! Then maybe I'll consider moving!"

__7__ facts dealing with or using numbers	__6__ husband or wife
__8__ equally balanced, distributed	__3__ old
__1__ more than necessary	__4__ desiring; wanting very much
__9__ too many; too much	__5__ large amount in small area
__2__ unusual	

6/12

4 TASK LISTENING

Look at the map of the United States on the next page. In this report, you will hear four regions mentioned, as well as the nine states and one district highlighted in bold print.

Listen to the report and place a check (✔) on the name of the state or district when you hear it.

1980 census

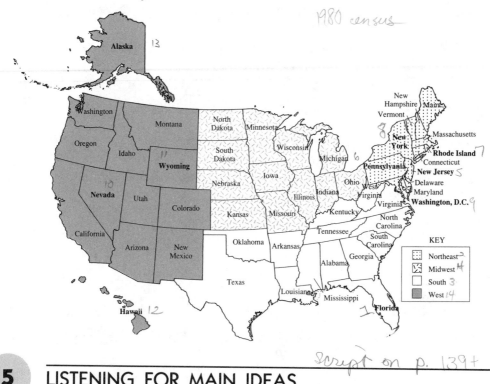

KEY

⊡ Northeast 2
☒ Midwest 4
☐ South 3
▨ West 14

Script on p. 139+

5 LISTENING FOR MAIN IDEAS

Listen to the report again. The report has been divided into three parts. You will hear a beep at the end of each part. As you listen, circle the answer that best expresses the main idea in that part. Compare your answers with those of another student.

PART 1 What does the reporter say about men and women in the United States?

  a. More men live in the United States than women.
  b. Women and men are spread evenly in some states.
  c. Men and women are not spread evenly across the U.S.

PART 2 Which statement is true concerning the number of women living in the United States?

  a. The Northeast has the highest concentration of women.
  b. The South has the highest concentration of women.
  c. The Midwest has the highest concentration of women.

PART 3 Which statement is true concerning the number of men living in the United States?

    a. The Northeast has the highest concentration of men.

    b. The West has the highest concentration of men.

    c. The South has the highest concentration of men.

6 | LISTENING FOR DETAILS

Read the questions for Part 1. Then listen to Part 1 again. As you listen, circle the best answer. Compare your answers with those of another student. If you disagree, listen to Part 1 again.

PART 1

1. If you have been unlucky in love, your problem may be

    a. your personality.

    b. your breath.

    c. statistical.

2. Which of the following is true?

    a. Most Americans move a lot to meet men or women.

    b. Statistics are easy to give on the radio.

    c. There are generally more women than men in America.

Repeat the same procedure for Parts 2 and 3.

PART 2

3. The message in the song is that

    a. everybody should have a mate.

    b. every state should have the same number of men and women.

    c. women are longing to move.

4. Which states have more women than men?

   a. States with elderly populations

   b. States with longer summers

   c. Agricultural states

5. In which two places are men most rare?

   a. New Jersey and Pennsylvania

   b. Pennsylvania and Rhode Island

   c. New York and the District of Columbia

6. How do the black and white populations compare in the U.S.?

   a. They have the same ratio of boys and girls.

   b. They have a different ratio of boys and girls.

   c. White males die earlier than black males.

PART 3

7. Where are there more men than women in the U.S.?

   a. Where more boys than girls are born

   b. In most states

   c. In only four states

8. Which state has the most men for every 100 women?

   a. Nevada

   b. Hawaii

   c. Alaska

9. Why are there more men in the West than in the East?

   a. Because the gold rush produced more boys

   b. Because the *Wall Street Journal* advertises jobs there

   c. Because men find more jobs there

10. Which is *not* a job that men usually find in the West?

   a. Mining

   b. Clerical work

   c. Agricultural work

Class 6/12

7   LOOKING AT LANGUAGE   Comparative

Exercise 1

Listen again to the song about where the girls and boys are. Fill in the missing words.

For every being of the ___male___ sex,
1

___Fish___ or fowl or Tyrannosaurus rex,
2

For every being there should be a ___mate___,
3

But that's not ___so___ in every state.
4

Where the girls ___are___,
5

Where there's *more* called "___she___"
6

than there are called "he,"

Where the girls are,

That's the place that we're ___longing___ to be.
7

For every being of the female ___sex___,
8

Fish or ___fowl___ or Tyrannosaurus rex,
9

For every being there ___should___ be a mate,
10

But that's not so in ___every___ state.
11

Where the ___boys___ are,
12

Where there's *more* called "he"

than there are called "___she___,"
13

___Where___ the boys are,
14

That's the ___place___ that we're longing to be.
15

Work with another student. Discuss the use of the words in italics. What is being compared in these examples?

Explanation

In the above examples, the number of men and women is being compared. The comparison in the first example could be written more completely as:

> There are *more people* called "she" *than* there are people called "he" in many states.
>
> or
>
> There are *fewer people* called "he" *than* there are people called "she" in many states.

These examples compare a countable noun: *people*. You can also compare adjectives. For example:

> Alaska is *greater in size than* New York.
> New York is *smaller in size than* Alaska.

In these two examples, the adjectives *great* and *small* are short adjectives. They form the comparison by adding *-er*. Adjectives with two or more syllables form the comparison with *more* or *less*. For example:

> New York is *more populated than* Alaska.
>
> or
>
> Alaska is *less populated than* New York.

Exercise 2

Class 6/12

Read the following summary of the report. Fill in the blanks with the correct form of the comparative. The first one has been done for you.

If you're looking for a mate, some states may be

<u>more interesting</u> to live in _____<u>than</u>_____ others. Women and
(interesting)   1

men are not spread evenly across the United States. There

are some regions where there are more men than women

and others where there are _____ women

_____ men.
   2

In America, as a whole, the population of women is

_____ _____ the population of men.
(large)   3
Therefore, many states have a _____ abundance
(great)
of women _____ men to begin with.
4

Jobs have an effect on the spread of population. For example, the southern and eastern parts of the United States have a _____ concentration of women
(high)
_____ the western parts because there are
5
_____ clerical and retail jobs there_____
6
in other areas. In contrast, there are _____ jobs in mining and agriculture in the southern and eastern parts _____there are in the western parts. Consequently,
7
we find that men are _____ in some of the
8 (concentrated)
western states.

Age is another factor which affects the distribution of male and female populations. In general, women live longer than men. Southern states, like Florida, which are _____ _____ the northeastern or
(warm)   9
midwestern states, are usually _____ with the
10 (populated)
elderly. As a result, there are _____ women _____ men in those states.
11

Consequently, if you're having trouble meeting the right boyfriend or girlfriend, think about where the boys and girls are before your next move!

8 FOLLOW-UP ACTIVITIES

Discussion Questions

In groups, discuss your answers to the following questions.

1. Why do certain jobs attract more men than women, or more women than men? Are the examples in the report the same in your country? Have sex-associated jobs changed in recent years? How?
2. How can you meet someone of the opposite sex when the ratio of men and women is not favorable?

Essay Topics

Choose one of the following topics.

1. Compare two places where you have lived. Describe the advantages and disadvantages of living and working in each place.
2. The gold rush was a period in American history when many men (and some women) moved west in great numbers, hoping to become rich with the discovery of gold. This movement of people changed the spread of population across the United States.

   Was there a period in the history of your country in which a sudden change in the spread of population occurred? Write an essay in which you describe how and why the change happened.

Values Clarification   The Best Place to Live and Work

Work in small groups. Imagine that you are looking for a job. You have found job openings in five states. The salaries offered differ in each state. However, each salary corresponds to the cost of living in that state. You are willing to move, but the quality of life is important to you. You want to choose the state that will offer you the best life.

Read the following descriptions. Each person in your group should rank the states in the order of the "most desirable" (#1) to the "least desirable" (#5) state to live in. Compare your choices with the others in your group and try to agree on the ranking.

Handwritten annotations:

* make up similar descriptions for various regions of Japan:
Hokkaido, Tohoku, Hokuriku, Chubu, Kanto, Kansai, Chugoku, Kinki, Kyushu, Shikoku.

(include the prefectures which are in these areas, and big cities)

note one historical event from each area.

NEW JERSEY
New Jersey, the Garden State, is famous for its beaches and historical sights. The four distinct seasons attract tourists from near and far. New Jersey is close to New York City, so many residents of this state can enjoy a metropolitan lifestyle. Because of growing businesses and the need for clerical workers, there are more women than men living in this state.

RHODE ISLAND
This state is located in New England. It is well known for its history. Many parts of the state are quite rustic, and there are beautiful historic houses along the ocean. There are many fine beaches. The state is popular among the very rich in the summer. It is located near Boston, one of the most historic cities on the east coast. There are more women than men living in Rhode Island.

HAWAII
This state consists of several small islands. There is a strong Polynesian influence in Hawaii because of its geographic location in the Pacific Ocean. The state is quite separate from the other U.S. states. There is a warm climate and an interesting marine life which attracts many tourists to the state. The cost of living is quite high. There are more men than women living in this state.

FLORIDA
This state has a warm climate and is famous for its beaches. It is a favorite family vacation spot. There are many hotels and resorts because of the state's wonderful climate. There is a strong Spanish influence, from both the history of the state and its current Hispanic population. Because of its warm climate, many elderly people move to the state when they stop working. There are more women than men living in this state, primarily because of its older female population.

ALASKA
Alaska is known for its wildlife, glaciers, and salmon fishing. Cross-country skiing and hiking are popular sports in this state. The winters are long and cold, but the summers are pleasant, with many hours of sunlight. The male population is much greater than the female population. There is a large Indian and Eskimo population living in Alaska. The cost of living is quite high in this state, but salaries are comparable.

"Where the Girls and Boys Are" was first broadcast on *All Things Considered*, August 22, 1983. The reporter is Robert Krulwich.

THE THINKING CAP

1 PREDICTING

From the title, discuss what you think the interview is about.

2 THINK AHEAD

In groups, discuss your answers to the following questions.

1. When do you do your best thinking? When do you feel most creative? What helps you to be more creative?
2. Have you ever wanted to invent something on your own? What was it? How did you get the idea?
3. What would you like to see invented?

3 VOCABULARY

The words in italics will help you understand the interview. Read the following sentences. Try to guess the meaning of these words from the context of the sentences. Then write a synonym or your own definition of the words.

1. Many people like to live in warm climates. However, when the temperature reaches 95 to 100 *degrees*, some feel it's much too hot.

_____

2. Some of the best discoveries are made because people *stumble on* them by accident.

_____

3. When a child is sick and feels hot, his mother can often tell if he has a *fever* just with the touch of her hand.

_____

4. Touching a person's *forehead* will usually tell you whether or not he or she has a high temperature.

_____

5. A *heating pad* can help take away pain. If a part of your body hurts, its warming effect can sometimes help.

_____

6. Heating pads have heating *elements* in them. These elements make the pad warm.

_____

7. If you drive a motorcycle, you should wear a *helmet* to protect your head in case of an accident.

_____

8. When a scientist discovers something new, he or she must test it many times to *prove* that it works.

_____

9. Scientists and inventors often ask private companies or the government to *fund* them in their work. This is because their work is often very expensive.

_____

10. Many people put their money in a bank where the interest on their money is *compounded* daily. This way, the value of their money increases very quickly.

_____

11. In today's world, many people have several *tasks* to do in one day: work, shop, cook, and clean. It's not easy to find the time to do them all.

_____

Now try to match the words with a definition or synonym. Then compare your answers with those of another student. The first one has been done for you.

__e__ 1. degrees   a. something used to warm part of the body

____ 2. stumble on   b. small jobs

____ 3. fever   c. protection for the head

____ 4. forehead   d. part of the face above the eyes

____ 5. heating pad   e. measurements for temperature

____ 6. elements   f. high body temperature

____ 7. helmet   g. added

____ 8. prove   h. electrical wires

____ 9. fund   i. test, or show something is true

____10. compounded   j. find unexpectedly

____11. tasks   k. give money

4 TASK LISTENING

Listen to the interview. Find the answer to the following question.

> **What does "The Thinking Cap" do to the brain?**

5 LISTENING FOR MAIN IDEAS

Listen to the interview again. The interview has been divided into four parts. You will hear a beep at the end of each part. As you listen, circle the answer that best expresses the main idea in that part. Compare your answers with those of another student.

PART 1   How was "The Thinking Cap" invented?

     a. Edward Brainard was looking for inspiration.

     b. Edward Brainard was talking with friends.

     c. Edward Brainard thought of it by accident.

PART 2 What effect does "The Thinking Cap" have on people?

    a. It helps people cook.

    b. It gives people a fever.

    c. It makes people more creative.

PART 3 How was "The Thinking Cap" made?

    a. Edward Brainard put heating pads together.

    b. Edward Brainard's son, David, created it.

    c. Edward Brainard used his motorcycle helmet.

PART 4 What effect did "The Thinking Cap" have on people?

    a. People could do mathematical computations faster.

    b. People could make more money when they wore it.

    c. People could travel more comfortably when they wore it.

6 LISTENING FOR DETAILS

Read the statements for Part 1. Then listen to Part 1 again and decide whether the statements are true or false. As you listen, write a *T* or *F* next to each statement. Compare your answers with those of another student. If you disagree, listen to Part 1 again.

PART 1

_____ 1. In search of inspiration, some people take walks.

_____ 2. Edward Brainard is from Massachusetts.

_____ 3. "The Thinking Cap" warms the brain by eight degrees.

_____ 4. Edward Brainard was in an accident.

Repeat the same procedure for Parts 2, 3, and 4.

PART 2

_____ 5. In 1974, Edward Brainard had four children at home.

_____ 6. His son David usually cooked supper.

_____ 7. The "Thinking Cap" gives people a fever.

_____ 8. Edward thought that heating the head would make people think faster.

_____ 9. He decided to try heating the human head.

PART 3

_____10. Edward made the cap by taping together two heating pads.

_____11. The cap covers all of the forehead.

_____12. Edward created the cap over his wife's head.

_____13. Edward felt where the elements should go on his head.

_____14. "The Heated Helmet" is the same as "The Thinking Cap."

PART 4

_____15. Edward Brainard was sure that his thinking had improved.

_____16. He was scared to tell anybody about it.

_____17. Edward Brainard has proven that "The Thinking Cap" works.

_____18. Some bankers wear "The Thinking Cap."

_____19. Edward Brainard thinks that a person can do more tasks each day with "The Thinking Cap."

_____20. He will market "The Thinking Cap" next year.

7 · LOOKING AT LANGUAGE Present Unreal Conditional

Exercise 1

Listen to the following segment of the interview. Focus on the verb forms in italics. What is Edward Brainard saying about earning money?

> "You have to think in terms of compounding money in a bank. If you *were* always one percent . . . (doing one percent) better than the other person compounding money, after ten years you*'d be* way, way ahead."

Explanation

In this example, Edward Brainard compares doing computations with "The Thinking Cap" to compounding money in a bank. He imagines what would happen if we were compounding money in a bank and did one percent better than another person.

We use the present unreal conditional when we want to imagine a situation in the present or describe something which is *not* real and make a statement about it.

Exercise 2

Look at the following example and answer the questions. If we *wore* thinking caps in school, we *would think* faster and *be* more creative.

1. What is the verb form in the conditional clause "if we wore thinking caps in school"?
2. What is the verb form in the result clause "we would think faster and be more creative"?

Practice the present unreal conditional in the following sentences. Imagine that you are going to wear "The Thinking Cap." Complete the sentences with the correct verb form. The first one has been done for you.

1. If I ___*needed*___ (need) to get a job done in just a few hours, I *would put on* (put on) a thinking cap before work.

2. If I _____ (have to) take an exam, I _____ (wear) the thinking cap the night before the exam.

3. I _____ (use) "The Thinking Cap" if I _____ (want) to do mathematical computations faster.

4. If I _____ (raise) the temperature of "The Thinking Cap" by 5 degrees, the speed of my thinking _____ (increase) even more.

5. If stores _____ (sell) "Thinking Caps," many people _____ (buy) them to improve their thinking.

Exercise 3

Now write four sentences about better thinking or creativity. Complete the following sentences. Use the present unreal conditional.

1. If I wanted to be more creative, _____

_____.

2. _____

if I needed to pass an important exam.

3. _____,

I would invent one.

4. If I were a scientist, _____

_____.

8 FOLLOW-UP ACTIVITIES

Discussion Questions

In groups, discuss your answers to the following questions.

1. Would you buy "The Thinking Cap"? Why or why not?
2. Edward Brainard said that doing mathematical computations one percent faster is significant. Do you agree with him? Why or why not?
3. What kind of people might buy "The Thinking Cap"?

Essay Topics

Choose one of the following topics.

1. People are always trying to improve thinking. Edward Brainard says that when people wear "The Thinking Cap", they think faster and are more creative. It has also been said that eating protein before an exam helps students perform better.

    Can thinking be improved? Write an essay in which you express your opinions. Be sure to use examples from your own experience to explain your point of view.
2. What is creativity? Are people more creative today, or were they more creative in the past? Write an essay in which you discuss your concept of creativity. Use examples to support your point of view.

Design A Product to Improve Thinking

In the interview, you heard about "The Thinking Cap", a heated helmet which improves people's thinking. Edward Brainard found this idea "by accident" when he was talking to his son about a fever.

Work in groups. Invent a product which will help improve people's thinking. Prepare a description of your invention. In preparing, consider the following:

- the materials you will use for your invention
- how it will work
- how you will test it
- how and when it will be used
- whether you will market it and how

Present your invention to the rest of the class.

"The Thinking Cap" was first broadcast on *Morning Edition*, February 16, 1985. The interviewer is Alex Chadwick.

WHO IS MORE AFRAID OF NUCLEAR WAR?

1 PREDICTING

From the title, discuss what you think the interview is about.

2 THINK AHEAD

Work in groups. Read the following statements. Do you agree with them? See if everyone in your group has the same opinion.

1. Americans are more afraid of nuclear war than Russians.
2. A nuclear war is likely in our lifetime.
3. Most people would probably survive a nuclear war.
4. A country attacked by a nuclear bomb should fight back.
5. Life will be better for our children than it is for us.

3 VOCABULARY

The words in italics will help you understand the interview. Read the text. Try to guess the meaning of these words. Then match the words with their definitions or synonyms in the list at the end of the text. Write the number of each word next to its definition or synonym. Compare your answers with those of another student. The first one has been done for you.

Many people in North America, as in the rest of the world, are worried about the possibility of a nuclear war. They are worried about their future because they believe that it will be difficult for the world powers to avoid a nuclear war. In fact, some families in North America have made difficult choices because of this fear. For example, some couples in the United States have decided not to have children; they believe the world is no longer a safe place to raise a family. In Canada, some families are moving away from big cities because of their fear of nuclear war. They are moving to the distant *provinces* because they feel that, in case of nuclear war, they will be safer in these areas.

How do these people know what will happen in the future? No one knows where the nuclear arms race will go. No one knows for sure if a country will ever really use a nuclear bomb. Would a powerful country ever decide to drop a nuclear bomb on another country? And would an attacked country ever decide to *retaliate*? Would it drop a bomb on the country that had attacked it? No one has definite answers to these questions, but many people seem to have *theories* about the world's future.

Unfortunately, many of these theories are not very positive. Why aren't people more *optimistic* about their future? What has influenced some people to make such extreme choices in their lives?

The *mass media* has certainly had a lot to do with the way people view the world. Every day, television reports and radio interviews focus on the problems in the world. It's not easy to ignore the depressing pictures that are shown on TV. Every day natural *disasters*, accidents, and crimes are shown to the public. Little information is *edited*; the public can see everything that happens, as often as it is happening.

Newspapers are another form of mass media that influences our thinking. We can often read what the general public thinks about an issue. For example, more and more *opinion polls* are *administered* to find out how people feel about their future. These polls try to get a typical example of public opinion by interviewing a *cross section* of people. These general responses are then published in the newspapers. The results of these polls may also influence our own thinking.

The mass media seems to have an important role in forming people's views of the world. One wonders how this role will affect us in the future. Will people form opinions based on the mass media's representation of the world? Or, will they receive information objectively and come to their own conclusions about the future?

8 survey

9 given; handed out

4 expecting the best; feeling positive about things

2 give back the same bad treatment that one has received

3 explanations not necessarily based on fact

5 newspapers, radio, TV, and other ways of providing information

6 terrible accidents

7 changed; left out

10 a part or group that is typical of the whole

1 large regions of a country

57

4 TASK LISTENING

Listen to the interview. Find the answer to the following question.

> Which countries participated in this opinion poll? *U.s/Russia*

5 LISTENING FOR MAIN IDEAS

Listen to the interview again. The interview has been divided into five parts. You will hear a beep at the end of each part. Circle the answer which best expresses the main idea in that part. Compare your answers with those of another student.

PART 1 What did a recent opinion poll show?

    a. Russian teenagers fear nuclear war less than American teenagers.

    b. American teenagers fear nuclear war less than Russian teenagers.

    c. Russian and American teenagers fear nuclear war equally.

PART 2 How did the teenagers feel about surviving a nuclear war?

    a. The Russians were more optimistic than the Americans.

    b. The Americans were more optimistic than the Russians.

    c. The American and Russian students felt the same.

PART 3 How did the Russian and American students feel about the future of their children?

    a. The Russians were more optimistic than the Americans.

    b. The Americans were more optimistic than the Russians.

    c. The Russians and Americans felt the same.

PART 4 Why do Russian youths feel the way they do, according to Jonathon Tudge?

    a. They don't know very much about nuclear war.

    b. They don't believe a nuclear war could happen.

    c. They don't believe the disasters they see on TV.

PART 5 How do Mr. Robinson and Mr. Tudge feel about their poll?

     a. They feel that they should have taken a national survey.
     b. They feel that they have a good representative sample.
     c. They are unhappy with their questions.

6   LISTENING FOR DETAILS

Read the statements for Part 1. Then listen to Part 1 again and decide whether the statements are true or false. As you listen, write a *T* or *F* next to each statement. Compare your answers with those of another student. If you disagree, listen to Part 1 again.

PART 1

   _T_ 1. The Soviets and Americans administered a joint opinion poll.

   _T_ 2. Americans had never administered an opinion poll in the Soviet Union before.

   _F_ 3. Teenagers were interviewed across America.

   _F_ 4. The teenagers were in tenth grade.

   _T_ 5. In Russia, over 2,000 teenagers were interviewed.

   _T_ 6. The Russians were interviewed in two regions.

Repeat the same procedure for Parts 2, 3, 4, and 5.

PART 2

   _F_ 7. Most teenagers in both countries thought they would be able to survive a nuclear war. not

   _T_ 8. More Russians agreed with retaliation than Americans.

PART 3

   _T_ 9. Seventy-five percent of the Soviets thought that life would be better for their children than for themselves.

   _T_ 10. Fifty percent of the Americans thought that life would be better for their children than for themselves.

PART 4

T 11. Russian children know about the realities of nuclear war.

F 12. Because of what they know about nuclear war, Russian children believe it is likely to happen. *not*

T 13. Russian children believe that their leaders would never let a nuclear war happen.

F 14. The mass media focuses on disasters in Russia. *good thing*

F 15. Most Soviet television viewers are aware that television is edited. *no*

T 16. Mr. Tudge thinks most Russians accept what they are told without thinking about it.

PART 5

T 17. Mr. Robinson polled students in just one state.

T 18. He thinks that kids in Maryland will react the same as kids in Nebraska or California.

T 19. The answers given to the Maryland survey were similar to answers given to a national survey.

F 20. Mr. Tudge felt the two Russian provinces were perfectly representative of Russian opinion. *European Russ*

7 LOOKING AT LANGUAGE Reported Speech

Exercise 1

In reporting Russian and American teenagers' answers to their survey, Jonathon Tudge and John Robinson used both quotes and reported speech.

Listen to the following segment of the interview. In this statement, Jonathon Tudge directly quotes what some Russian children said when asked about the possibility of nuclear war.

Russian children know an awful lot about what is likely to happen if there were to be a nuclear war. And, because they know so much about it, they feel it can't possibly happen. Over and over again, when you talk to Russian children, they *answer* this, things like, "*Our* leaders *will* never *let* it happen."

How would Jonathon Tudge report the children's answer if he did not use direct quotes?

Explanation

In reporting this statement, we would say:

Russian children *answered* that *their* leaders *would* never *let* it happen.

In reporting speech that took place in the past, the verbs are usually changed to a past form. In this example, *answer* becomes *answered*, and *will* becomes *would*. The possessive pronoun also changes in reported speech. In this example, *our* becomes *their*.

Exercise 2

The survey that Jonathon Tudge and John Robinson conducted could have had the following questions and answers, based on the results they reported.

Read the following questions and answers. Then write each student's answer in reported speech. Make the necessary changes of verb form and pronoun reference. The first one has been done for you.

1. (Question to an American male student)
   "*Do you think that there will be a nuclear war?*"
   "*Yes. I think a nuclear war is very likely.*"
   Reported statement:

   He said that he thought a nuclear war was very likely.

2. (Question to a group of Russian male students)
   "*Do you think that there will be a nuclear war?*"
   "*No. Our leaders will never let it happen.*"
   Reported statement:

3. (Question to an American female student)
   "Do you think you would be able to survive a nuclear war?"
   "No. I don't believe anyone can survive a nuclear war."
   Reported statement:

   _____

4. (Question to a group of Russian female students)
   "Do you think you would be able to survive a nuclear war?"
   "No. It's not possible to survive a nuclear war!"
   Reported statement:

   _____

5. (Question to a Russian female student)
   "In the case of nuclear war, do you believe in retaliation?"
   "Yes. Retaliation is the only way to deal with an attack."
   Reported statement:

   _____

6. (Question to a group of American male students)
   "In the case of nuclear war, do you believe in retaliation?"
   "Yes. We think retaliation is probably necessary."
   Reported statement:

   _____

7. (Question to a Russian male student)
   "Do you think life will be better for your children than it is for you?"
   "Yes. I definitely think it will be better for them."
   Reported statement:

   _____

8. (Question to American female students)
   "Do you think life will be better for your children than it is for you?"
   "No. Our children's lives will probably not be as good as our lives."
   Reported statement:

   _____

8 FOLLOW-UP ACTIVITIES

Discussion Questions

In groups, discuss your answers to the following questions.

1. There has been a great deal of focus on the superpowers in discussing nuclear war issues. Have other countries had enough say in the decisions regarding nuclear arms?
2. Jonathon Tudge said that Russian children are less afraid of nuclear war because they know more about it. Do you think that knowing more about a fearful event helps you fear it less? Give examples from your own experience.

Essay Topics

Choose one of the following topics.

1. In the interview, Jonathon Tudge said that the mass media in Russia focuses more on the good side of life than on disasters. However, much of the information is edited. In contrast, the American mass media often focuses on disasters, and it is often criticized for this.

   What role should the mass media have in presenting information about nuclear arms and the dangers of nuclear war? Write an essay in which you express your opinions.
2. In some American schools, teachers have begun educating children about the possibilities of nuclear war. Should it be the responsibility of the school to educate students about this problem? Write an essay in which you express your opinion.

Conducting a Survey   Nuclear War

Work in groups. Write a questionnaire. Write five *yes/no* questions that will ask people's opinions about nuclear war. Your group will interview a cross section of people. Decide where and when you will conduct the survey, how many people you will question, who they will be, etc.

When you take your survey, count the *yes* and *no* responses. Take notes on the interesting comments that people make. The following grid can be used to write your questions, count responses, and record comments.

Questions	Yes	No	Comments
Example: *Do you think that there will be a nuclear war?* 1.	//	HH I	*Our leaders will never let it happen.*
2.			
3.			
4.			
5.			

ORAL REPORT

When your group meets again, summarize the information you have collected from each question. Prepare an oral report to present to the rest of the class. Be sure to include an introduction to your survey, a summary of the results you have collected, and a conclusion. The conclusion should include your own interpretation of the information you collected.

ORAL PRESENTATION PROCEDURES

1. The first student introduces the group and gives an introduction to the survey that was conducted.
2. The next few students present one or two of the questions that were asked, statistics or general responses that were received, and interesting comments that were made

by the people who were interviewed. The comments mentioned should help explain why people answered the way they did.

3. The last student concludes the presentation by summarizing the information from the survey, interpreting it, and perhaps reacting to the results. (For example, "We were surprised to learn that most people thought . . .")

USEFUL WORDS AND PHRASES

When you talk about the people who answered your survey, you can call them:

- interviewees
- respondents

When you report the information you collected, you can begin:

- They agreed that . . .
- They stated that . . .
- They felt that . . .
- They believed that . . .

When you indicate the number of people surveyed, you can say:

- More than half agreed that . . .
- Almost three-quarters said that . . .
- Less than a third said that . . .
- Over 50 percent of the sample stated that . . .

"Who Is More Afraid of Nuclear War?" was first broadcast on *All Things Considered*, April 10, 1987. The interviewer is Renee Montaigne.

AT THE TABLE

1 **PREDICTING**

From the title, discuss what you think the interview is about.

2 THINK AHEAD

Work in groups. Read the following statements. Do you agree with them? See if everyone in your group has the same opinion.

1. A man should always wear a jacket and tie in a nice restaurant.
2. You should always brush your teeth before you go out.
3. A dinner table should have candles or flowers on it.
4. Champagne is better than wine.

3 VOCABULARY

The words in italics will help you understand the interview. Read the following sentences. Try to guess the meaning of these words from the context of the sentences. Then write a synonym or your own definition of the words.

1. Some parents spend a lot of time teaching their children good *manners*. They want them to have good behavior at the dinner table and in public.

_____

2. If you do not wear gloves when you plant flowers in the dirt, you will have dirty hands and *fingernails*.

_____

3. Men who like a *casual* life-style don't worry about wearing a suit and tie every day.

_____

4. Driving at night is difficult. Lights from oncoming cars can *impair* the driver's *vision*.

_____

5. Little children love to play the game of *peek-a-boo*, hiding from adults and then looking around the corner for attention.

_____

6. When you drink out of a glass, your lips touch the *rim* of the glass.

_____

7. City streets are often dirty and *unsanitary* because garbage is left on them.

_____

8. Wine glasses look more elegant than regular drinking glasses because they have long *stems*.

_____

9. A quick way to wipe your mouth is to *dab* it with a napkin.

_____

10. People who are overly concerned about small problems are sometimes referred to as *neurotic*.

_____

11. If red wine or tomato sauce gets on your clothes, you will have trouble getting them clean; the *stain* from these foods is difficult to wash out.

_____

Now try to match the words and expressions with a definition or synonym. Then compare your answers with those of another student. The first one has been done for you.

_c_ 1. manners   a. make it difficult to see

_i_ 2. fingernails   b. overly worried about things

_k_ 3. casual   c. habits or behaviors

_a_ 4. impair vision   d. not clean; not healthy

_h_ 5. peek-a-boo   e. top of a glass

_e_ 6. rim   f. touch lightly and gently

_d_ 7. unsanitary   g. thin bottom part of a wine glass

_g_ 8. stem   h. small child's hiding game

_f_ 9. dab   i. the hard ends of the fingers

_b_ 10. neurotic   j. dirty mark or color

_j_ 11. stain   k. informal

4 TASK LISTENING

Listen to the interview. You will hear examples of Craig Claiborne's opinion on manners. As you listen, check the things that he talks about.

____ dirty fingernails   ____ candles on the table

____ clean shirts   ____ flowers on the table

____ brushing teeth   ____ wine service

____ talking at the table   ____ food service

5   LISTENING FOR MAIN IDEAS

Listen to the interview again. The interview has been divided into three parts. You will hear a beep at the end of each part. Circle the answer which best expresses the main idea in that part. Compare your answers with those of another student.

1. What is Craig Claiborne's opinion about people at the table?

   a. He says we eat the wrong food.

   b. He feels our manners are generally good.

   c. He is worried about our manners.

2. How does Craig Claiborne think we should behave at the table?

   a. We should be very proper.

   b. We should be very casual.

   c. We should do special things.

3. What is his concern about wine?

   a. People order the wrong wines at the wrong time.

   b. People don't drink, serve, or talk about wine properly.

   c. People drink too much wine when they go out.

6   LISTENING FOR DETAILS

Read the statements for Part 1. Then listen to Part 1 again and decide whether the statements are true or false. As you listen, write a *T* or *F* next to each statement. Compare your answers with those of another student. If you disagree, listen to Part 1 again.

PART 1

___F___ 1. Craig Claiborne had several weeks of summer vacation.

___T___ 2. He works for the *New York Times*.

___F___ 3. He sees a decline in our manners.

Repeat the same procedure for Parts 2 and 3.

PART 2

Craig Claiborne says he . . .

___T___ 4. would never go out in public with dirty fingernails.

___F___ 5. would not go out without brushing his teeth.

___F___ 6. leads a very formal lifestyle.

According to Craig Claiborne, you should . . .

___F___ 7. never put candles on a table.

___T___ 8. put only low flower arrangements on the table.

PART 3

According to Craig Claiborne, you should . . .

___F___ 9. always hold a wine glass by the rim.

___T___ 10. hold a good wine glass by the stem.

___T___ 11. wipe your lips each time you drink some wine.

___F___ 12. not order champagne at dinner.

___F___ 13. let wine drip on the label when you pour it.

___T___ 14. show your guests the wine before you serve it.

LOOKING AT LANGUAGE A Modal of Advice

Exercise 1

Listen again to the statements made by Craig Claiborne in the interview. Each statement gives his advice on table manners.

Craig Claiborne:

You should never put a candle . . . candles on a table that will impair the flow of vision. If you and I are sitting across from each other, the candles should be so low that you and I can look at each other, in each other's eyes, without being . . . having our vision marred by the candle flame.

Interviewer:

And what about flowers? Same thing?

Craig Claiborne:

The same thing is true. You should always have . . . if you have flowers on the table, there should be an arrangement low enough so that you and I don't have to peek-a-boo, looking around the flower arrangement to see each other.

Underline the modal Craig Claiborne uses each time he gives us advice. Discuss the form of the verb which follows this modal.

Explanation

Notice that Craig Claiborne uses *should* when he wants to give radio listeners advice. He is saying, "In my opinion, I think it is good for you to do this when you are at the table."

Exercise 2

Work with another student. Your partner is planning to visit your country, and is not familiar with the eating customs there. Use *should, shouldn't, should always,* or *should never* to give advice on the following topics:

- when to begin eating
- refusing to eat what you are served
- talking while eating
- smacking your lips or licking your fingers
- putting your elbows on the table
- putting your hands on your lap
- yawning at the table
- leaving food on your plate
- excusing yourself from the table

Discuss other table manners that are important in your country.

8 FOLLOW-UP ACTIVITIES

Discussion Questions

In groups, discuss your answers to the following questions.

1. Do you agree with Craig Claiborne's advice on table manners? Why or why not?
2. If you had children, what table manners would you teach them? What are the "shoulds" and "should nots" of children's table manners in your country?

Essay Topics

Choose one of the following topics.

1. Imagine that you have invited a foreign friend to a wedding in your country. Your friend is concerned about the customs of your country. What do people wear? What kind of presents are given? What time do people arrive or leave? Who dances with whom, etc.?
   Write a letter to your friend. Give him or her advice on how to prepare for the wedding.
2. How are table manners and eating habits in the United States different from those in your country? Write an essay in which you compare and contrast the customs of the two countries.

Design A Book of Etiquette

In the early 1900s, Emily Post wrote a book of etiquette. The book consisted of the "shoulds" and "should nots" of living in "high society." For example, young women were told to always wear white gloves when they went to a dance. This was so that they would never touch a man's hand. Men were told to always walk on the street side of the sidewalk when they walked with a woman. This was so that the woman would not get dirty from the carriages driving by on the street.

The rules of etiquette have certainly changed since the early 1900s.

Work in small groups. Write a short book of etiquette for modern living. What are the things people "should do" or "should not do" in different social situations? Think about the following situations and write your rules of etiquette:

- table manners in a restaurant
- entertaining in the home
- dress for all occasions
- dating
- gift giving
- how to act at a party

"At the Table" was first broadcast on *Morning Edition*, July 12, 1987. The interviewer is Susan Stamberg.

FROM ONE WORLD TO ANOTHER

1 PREDICTING

From the title, discuss what you think the interview is about.

2 THINK AHEAD

In groups, discuss your answers to the following questions.

1. Did one of your parents influence your life an any special way? What was his or her influence on you?
2. Do you feel that you are a part of your neighborhood, school, or community? Why or why not?
3. What influences you the most in making choices: your cultural background, your sex, your role in your family?

3 VOCABULARY

The following words will help you understand the interview. Try to guess the meaning of the words. Use your knowledge of English, or use your dictionaries. In each set of words, cross out the word that does not have a similar meaning to the italicized word. Then compare your answers with those of another student. Discuss why these words are similar. The first one has been done for you.

1. *poetry*	poem	poet	~~poll~~
2. *dedicate*	devote	~~ignore~~	show thanks
3. *raise*	bring up	~~study~~	educate
4. *grow up*	~~produce~~	mature	develop
5. *reservation*	area	land	~~house~~
6. *connected to*	a part of	~~separate from~~	tied to
7. *exiled*	removed	separated	~~joined~~
8. *pore over*	~~glance at~~	study	look at carefully
9. *deal with*	manage	~~neglect~~	control
10. *heritage*	from parents	tradition	~~creation~~

4 TASK LISTENING

Listen to the interview. Find the answer to the following question.

> What is Roberta Hill Whiteman's cultural background?

Am Indian

5 LISTENING FOR MAIN IDEAS

Listen to the interview again. The interview has been divided into four parts. You will hear a beep at the end of each part. Choose the answer that best expresses the main idea in that part. Compare your answers with those of another student.

PART 1 Why did Roberta Hill Whiteman write the poem, "I'uni Kwi Athi? Hiatho."?

    a. The Mohawk Indians asked her to.
    b. She wanted to thank her father.
    c. She wanted to write for the reservation.

PART 2 How does Roberta Hill Whiteman feel about the two worlds she grew up in?

    a. They are very different.
    b. They are connected.
    c. They make one large community.

PART 3 Why does Roberta Hill Whiteman write poetry?

    a. Her grandmother asked her to.
    b. She can make a lot of money selling books.
    c. The language of poetry makes her feel good.

PART 4 What is an important symbol in her poetry?

    a. Nature
    b. Modern life
    c. Her father

LISTENING FOR DETAILS

Read the questions for Part 1. Then listen to Part 1 again. As you listen, circle the best answer. Compare your answers with those of another student. If you disagree, listen to Part 1 again.

PART 1

1. What does Roberta Hill Whiteman describe in her poem?

   a. White horses

   b. Leaves

   c. A new place

2. What else does she write about in her poem?

   a. An iced beer

   b. An ice bear

   c. A nice bird

3. Who did she dedicate the poem to?

   a. Her father

   b. The Oneida Indians

   c. Her mother

4. When did her father die?

   a. When she was very young

   b. In the late sixties

   c. In the early twenties

Repeat the same procedure for Parts 2, 3, and 4.

PART 2

5. Where did Roberta Hill Whiteman grow up?

   a. In Wisconsin

   b. 10 miles from Green Bay

   c. On the Oneida reservation

6. What does she say about the Oneida reservation?

   a. The people are nice there.

   b. The land is very rich there.

   c. There is a connection with the "long ago" there.

7. What happened to her as a child?

   a. She was exiled from the reservation.

   b. She began to understand the people around her.

   c. She didn't feel connected to people around her.

PART 3

8. What influences Roberta Hill Whiteman's poetry the most?

   a. Her role as a woman, mother, wife, and daughter.

   b. The stories that her grandmother wrote.

   c. Her grandmother's poetry books.

9. What does writing poetry do for her?

   a. It helps her to learn a new language.

   b. It helps her to make up her mind.

   c. It helps her to deal with things.

10. What did her grandmother make her pay attention to?

    a. Her social being

    b. Her mother

    c. Her voice through poetry

PART 4

11. What does Roberta Hill Whiteman describe in *Overcast Dawn*?

    a. Dreams

    b. Family

    c. Someone's death

12. What is special about her poems?

    a. Her description of natural things

    b. Her description of her father

    c. Her description of the reservation

13. What does the interviewer say about *Star Quilt*?

    a. It is her second collection of poetry.

    b. It is published in Minneapolis.

    c. It is written by Carolyn Forché.

7 LOOKING AT LANGUAGE Poetry

Exercise 1

Listen to Roberta Hill Whiteman read parts of two of her poems. Fill in the missing words.

I'uni Kwi Athi? Hiatho.

White horses, tails ___high___ , rise from the cedar.
1

___Smoke___ brings the fat crickets,
2

trembling breeze.

Find that holy place, a ___promise___ .
3

Embers glow like moon ___air___ .
4

. . . .

Will you _brush_ (5) my ear? An ice bear sometimes
lumbers _west_ (6).
Your life still gleams, the edge _melting_ (7).
I never let you _know_ (8).
You showed me how under _snow_ (9) and darkness,
grasses breathe for _miles_ (10).

Overcast Dawn

This _morning_ (11) I feel dreams dying.
One trace is this _feather_ (12)
fallen from a gull,
with its _broken_ (13) shaft,
slight white down,
and long _dark_ (14) tip
that won't hold _air_ (15).
How will you reach me
if all our _dreams_ (16) are dead?

. . . .

Analysis of Poems

Work in groups and answer the following questions.

1. The first poem, "I'uni Kwi Athi? Hiatho." was dedicated to Roberta Hill Whiteman's father. She said that she had never had a chance to thank him for raising her. After reading this poem, what do you think she is thanking her father for? What did he teach her?

2. The second poem's title is "Overcast Dawn". "Overcast" is a word we use to describe the sky when it is covered

with dark clouds. "Dawn" is the early part of the morning, the first light of the day. Why do you think the poet chose this title for this poem? Why "overcast"? Why "dawn"?

Exercise 2

Examine the language used in the poems. The language of poetry is not the same as the language we hear or read daily. Roberta Hill Whiteman's description of nature creates images. She said in the interview that she found in language ways to express the "pictures in her mind." A poet uses common words in new ways to create these "pictures." For example, in these poems, the word "moon" is used to create an image of the time of day. In other words, "moon" tells us that it is night time. Familiar words are placed in unexpected categories to build the pictures of poetry.

Under each category below, list the words from nature and the descriptive verbs that the poet uses in her two poems. One example from each category has been done for you.

Animals & Parts of the Body of an Animal	Plants	Time of Day	Weather	Descriptive Verbs
horses	*cedar*	*moon*	*breeze*	*trembling*

Exercise 3

Write your own poem using descriptive vocabulary from nature. Try to use words from the categories above to describe people, places, events, or feelings.

8   FOLLOW-UP ACTIVITIES

Discussion Questions

In groups, discuss your answers to the following questions.

1. Have you ever felt that you moved from one world to another? If so, why did you feel this way?
2. Roberta Hill Whiteman's father taught her to listen and pay attention. He influenced her poetry. She also mentions the influence that her grandmother's books had on her.

   How have your parents or other family members influenced you? What influence did books have on you as a child? How did these things contribute to who you are today?

Essay Topics

Choose one of the following topics.

1. In moving from one culture to another, people often feel exiled in their new environment. In your own experience, have you ever felt a loss of "connectedness" to your environment?

   Write an essay in which you describe the situation and how you felt.
2. Roberta Hill Whiteman said that she had never really thanked her father for raising her.

   Write a letter to a person whom you never thanked for something important.

Role-play   The Reservation

For this role-play, the class is divided into three groups. One group will prepare the points of view of Glenn Ryan, a Native American. Another group will prepare the points of view of his parents. A third group will prepare the points of view of his grandparents. Read the situation, choose roles, and after a fifteen-minute preparation, begin a family discussion.

THE SITUATION

Glenn Ryan is a native American Indian. He grew up on a reservation in the southwest of the United States. He has always felt connected to the people there. His family lives on the reservation, and they share their work on the land with other people living there. The sense of community is very strong because the people have a common heritage.

However, life on the reservation has many limitations. For example, when children grow up, they usually leave the reservation if they want to continue their education or find a good job. There isn't much opportunity for them on the reservation.

Glenn Ryan was a very good student in high school. His grades were high. Consequently, he was offered a four-year scholarship to study at Stanford University in California. He has been studying literature and economics in undergraduate school at Stanford for a year now.

Two weeks ago Glenn returned to the reservation for summer vacation. Reality has also returned. Many of his relatives are unemployed and poor. He feels ashamed and helpless because he is studying on a beautiful campus that he can go back to. He feels guilty that he can no longer help his family with their land on the reservation.

Glenn's return home has deeply affected him. He is thinking of not going back to school. He wants to remain on the reservation with his family because he knows that he could help them by working on the land. He could also get a part-time job off the reservation to bring in some extra money. He does not want to see them unhappy. Tomorrow he will talk with his family to decide whether he will return to school or stay and work on the reservation.

THE ROLES

GLENN RYAN

You don't want to travel between two worlds anymore. You don't feel connected to the university community. You feel you have lost your culture and identity at school. The people there are very different from you. You realize that an education is important, but your family is more important to you right now. You think that you can help build the reservation.

GLENN'S PARENTS

> You never had the opportunity to go to college. You believe that Glenn should not abandon his education. In your opinion, his education is the only way he can help the Native American culture. You understand Glenn's feelings, but want to convince him to go back to school. You believe he will come back to the reservation once he has completed his studies.

GLENN'S GRANDPARENTS

> You would like Glenn to come back to live on the reservation. You have seen too many young people leave the reservation; most of them do not come back. Your heritage has suffered over the years. You want Glenn to stay and help build the reservation and make it stronger. The reservation needs more young people on it. You are afraid that if Glenn goes back to school he will never want to come back to life on the reservation. You fear that he will forget his Native American heritage.

PROCEDURE FOR DISCUSSION

Form new groups to include at least one person playing each of the roles.

1. Glenn, his parents, and his grandparents meet. Each person presents his or her point of view to Glenn.
2. Glenn listens and reacts to the suggestions. Glenn's parents and grandparents also try to convince each other of their opinions.
3. After a fifteen- to twenty-minute discussion, Glenn decides whether to go back to school or stay on the reservation.
4. The group then compares Glenn's decision with the decision of the other groups in class.

"From One World to Another" was first broadcast on *All Things Considered*, October 24, 1984. The interviewer is Susan Stamberg.

TO FINISH FIRST

1 PREDICTING

From the title, discuss what you think the interview is about.

2 THINK AHEAD

In groups, discuss your answers to the following questions.

1. What sports are commonly practiced in your country?
2. In your country, which is more important in sports, competition or teamwork?
3. Do you think that winning is the most important thing in sports?

3 VOCABULARY

The words in italics will help you understand the interview. Read the text. Try to guess the meaning of these words. Then match the words with their definitions or synonyms in the list at the end of the text. Write the number of each word next to its definition or synonym. The first one has been done for you.

The Iditarod is a dogsled race that celebrates an event that happened in Alaska. In 1925, Alaskan dogs carried medicine from Anchorage to the faraway village of Nome. In Nome, many people were dying from a disease called *diphtheria*. At that time, dogsleds were used to travel long distances in Alaska, so *mushers* took the medicine to Nome by dogsled.

Today, many mushers enter the Iditarod race and follow the same *trail* from Anchorage to Nome. The Iditarod is not an easy race; many people do not even finish it. In fact, only a small percentage of mushers actually crosses the *finish line*. This is because during the race, the mushers experience too much *abuse* to their bodies: they get only a little sleep and they are physically tired. If they have to stop and *abandon* the race, they feel very frustrated because all their hard work preparing for the race *has gone down the drain.* It often takes months before they feel good again and can *get back into the swing of things.*

The dogs sometimes get sick and don't always finish the race either. In fact, this race is so dangerous to the health of the dogs that *veterinarians* have to be placed all along the trail. When they see a dog that is sick or too tired, they may suggest that the dog be dropped from the race and sent back to the city for rest. An exhausted dog will need *tons* of rest before it can get back into training. It's surprising how many people continue to enter this race year after year under such conditions!

_____ line which marks the end of a race

_____ bad treatment

_____ give up; leave behind

_____ track or path

_____ animal doctors

_____ dogsled drivers

_____ a lot

_____ is not worth the effort; is wasted effort

_____ go back to normal

_*1*_ serious disease

4 TASK LISTENING

Listen to the interview to find the answer to the following question.

> Did Susan Butcher win the race?

5 LISTENING FOR MAIN IDEAS

Listen to the interview again. The interview has been divided into five parts. You will hear a beep at the end of each part. Choose the answer which expresses the main idea in that part. Compare your answers with those of another student.

PART 1 What is said about Susan Butcher's dogsled race?

    a. She crossed the finish line.

    b. She was second after the winner this year.

    c. She had a cold and couldn't finish the race.

PART 2 How does Susan feel about losing?

    a. She's disappointed.

    b. She's angry.

    c. She's confused.

PART 3 What does Susan say about her dogs?

    a. Some of her dogs didn't finish the race.

    b. She abandoned some of her dogs.

    c. Veterinarians suggested she drop some dogs.

PART 4 How does Susan feel about the Iditarod race?

    a. It's worth it because she makes a lot of money.

    b. She gets little sleep and works hard.

    c. She thinks the dogs suffer too much.

PART 5 What are Susan's plans for future races?

    a. She says she'll take some time off.

    b. She doesn't want to work in the winter anymore.

    c. She plans to run again next year.

6 LISTENING FOR DETAILS

Read the statements in Part 1. Then listen to Part 1 again and decide whether the statements are true or false. As you listen, write a *T* or *F* next to each statement. Compare your answers with those of another student. If you disagree, listen to Part 1 again.

PART 1

_____ 1. Susan's dogs were disappointed that she didn't win the race.

_____ 2. Her team passed seventeen teams on the last day of the race.

_____ 3. Susan finished the 1983 Iditarod Race.

_____ 4. The run is 1,100 miles long.

_____ 5. Susan finished second in last year's race.

Repeat the same procedure for Parts 2 and 3.

PART 2

_____ 6. Susan feels tired because of the race's abuse to her body.

_____ 7. Each year Susan tolerates the abuse better.

_____ 8. Susan is disappointed about her position in the race.

_____ 9. In the first ten days of the race, Susan's team did well.

_____10. Susan got lost for eight hours.

_____11. Even though they got lost, Susan says her dogs kept their confidence.

PART 3

_____12. Susan had to leave fourteen dogs behind.

_____13. Now the dogs are back with Susan.

_____14. Veterinarians are located at every check point.

_____15. The mushers always decide when a dog should be dropped.

For Parts 4 and 5, listen and write the answers to the questions. Each answer will consist of a number concerning time, dates, or money.

PART 4

16. How much did Susan win from the race? _____

17. How much did Susan's training cost? _____
18. How many days after the leader did Susan finish the race? _____
19. How much sleep does a musher get each day? _____

20. How long do they mush the dogs? _____

21. How much rest do the dogs get? _____

PART 5

22. How much time did Susan think of taking off? _____
23. How many teams were still out on the trail during this interview? _____
24. How many years ago was the Iditarod started? _____
25. In which year did dogsled drivers try to help the problem of diphtheria in Alaska? _____

7 ## LOOKING AT LANGUAGE Noun Compounds

Exercise 1

Listen to the following statements from the interview. Discuss the use of the words in italics. Are they in the singular or plural form? Why?

1. "The Iditarod is an eleven hundred-*mile* or so, two-*week* run through Alaska from Anchorage up to Nome."

2. "They had had a local race there, called 'The Yukon Two Hundred,' a two hundred-*mile* race."

3. "A four-*hour* rest provides no rest for the mushers because we have to cook for them and feed them."

Explanation

A noun may be used as an adjective to modify another noun. The noun used as an adjective is always singular, even when preceded by a number. Look at the following phrases and notice the form of the modifying noun. It is often written as a hyphenated work.

1. an eleven hundred-mile run
2. a two-week run
3. a two hundred-mile race
4. a four-hour rest

Exercise 2

Complete the following sentences with a noun compound. The first one has been done for you.

1. A race which lasts two weeks is __*a*_____

   _*two-week race*_____.

2. A dogsled race which takes ten days is _____

   _____.

3. A rest which lasts for four hours is _____

   _____.

4. A prize which pays a musher who finishes the race

   thirty-two hundred dollars is _____

   _____.

5. A training which costs forty-thousand dollars is _____

   _____.

6. A dog team which has fourteen members is ————

————————————————————— .

7. A detour which lasts for eight hours is ——————

————————————————————— .

8 FOLLOW-UP ACTIVITIES

Discussion Questions

In groups, discuss your answers to the following questions.

1. What kinds of sports are competitive? What kinds of sports are not competitive? Which do you prefer? Why?
2. Would you compete in a race if you only won a little money? Should money be a factor in whether or not people compete in sports?

Essay Topics

Choose one of the following topics.

1. Have you ever been involved in a competitive sport? How did you feel about winning or losing? Write an essay in which you describe your experience.
2. Should some sports be limited to only men or only women? Write an essay in which you use examples to support your opinion.

Conducting a Survey Attitudes About Sports

Work in groups. Write a questionnaire. Write five *yes/no* questions that ask people's opinions about sports. Your group will interview a cross section of people. See pages 63–65 for specific procedures and useful words and phrases.

"To Finish First" was first broadcast on *All Things Considered*, March 23, 1983. The interviewer is Noah Adams.

MEET YOU ON THE AIR

1 PREDICTING

From the title, discuss what you think the interview is about.

2 THINK AHEAD

In groups, discuss your answers to the following questions.

1. What do you like to do on Saturday nights? Do you think it's important to go out?
2. How do men and women meet in your country?
3. Some Americans write personal ads to meet people. The following short advertisement is an example of a personal ad:

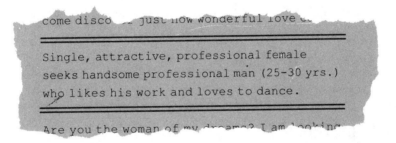

> come disco... just how wonderful love...
>
> Single, attractive, professional female
> seeks handsome professional man (25-30 yrs.)
> who likes his work and loves to dance.
>
> Are you the woman of my dreams? I am looking...

These people hope that someone will read their ad in a newspaper or magazine and be interested in meeting them. What do you think of this method of meeting people?

3 VOCABULARY

The following words will help you understand the interview. Try to guess the meaning of the words. Use your knowledge of English, or use your dictionaries. In each set of words, cross out the word that does not have a similar meaning. Then compare your answers with those of another student. Discuss why these words are similar. The first one has been done for you.

1. *date*	companion of the other sex	girlfriend/ boyfriend	~~place~~
2. *single*	unmarried	married	alone
3. *chat*	long discussion	small talk	short conversation

4. *match-maker*	person who arranges marriages	go-between	wife
5. *promote*	help	destroy	advertise
6. *banter*	playful talk	joking	argument
7. *sizzling*	cold	burning	passionate
8. *eccentric*	unusual	strange	average
9. *bland*	mild	uninteresting	outrageous

4 TASK LISTENING

Listen to the interview. You will hear different people talking. As you listen, check the subjects the people talk about.

_____ playing the piano   _____ looking for a job

_____ reading books   _____ eating Chinese food

_____ going to the beach   _____ drinking

5 LISTENING FOR MAIN IDEAS

Listen to the interview again. The interview has been divided into four parts. You will hear a beep at the end of each part. Choose the answer that best expresses the main idea in that part. Compare your answers with those of another student.

PART 1   What is "Date Night"?

    a. It's a radio show for singles.

    b. It's a new club for singles.

    c. It's a music show on the radio.

PART 2   How did "Date Night" get started?

    a.   Susan Block needed information to write a book.

    b.   Susan Block wanted to match up people on the air.

    c.   Radio listeners asked Susan Block to start it.

PART 3   How would you describe the conversations on the show?

    a.   Light-hearted conversations

    b.   Serious conservations

    c.   Debates about important topics

PART 4   According to Susan Block, why are the personal ads on this show better than personal ads in the paper?

    a.   They are edited more carefully.

    b.   They are more bland than the personals in the paper.

    c.   They give you a sense of the person's personality through their voice.

6   LISTENING FOR DETAILS

Read the questions for Part 1. Then listen to Part 1 again. As you listen, circle the best answer. Compare your answers with those of another student. If you disagree, listen to Part 1 again.

PART 1

1. Which of the following is *not* true about "Date Night?"

    a. It's a call-in show.

    b. It's in Los Angeles.

    c. It's a radio station.

2. What do people do after they meet on the air?

    a. They meet in town.

    b. They write to each other's box number.

    c. They become matchmakers.

3. Who is John?

   a. A matchmaker

   b. A famous musician

   c. Someone looking for a date

4. Who is Linda?

   a. The host of "Date Night"

   b. A woman who doesn't know what to do

   c. A person that John wants to talk to

Repeat the same procedure for Parts 2, 3, and 4.

PART 2

5. What did the show's host do?

   a. She wrote a book on how to play the personals.

   b. She wrote personal ads about herself.

   c. She called people who wrote personal ads.

6. What did Susan Block do on her talk show *before* "Date Night" started?

   a. She would make up personal ads for individuals.

   b. She expressed her feelings about dating on the air.

   c. She matched up single people who needed each other.

PART 3

7. What kind of banter is used on the show?

   a. The same as in a singles' bar

   b. The same as at work

   c. The same as in the movies

8. Which kind of Chinese food is *not* talked about?

   a. Sizzling chicken

   b. Hot and sour soup

   c. Stuffed dumplings

9. What does the man say you must do when you eat Chinese food?

    a. Take off your shoes

    b. Share your plates

    c. Use chop sticks

PART 4

10. What are personal ads on "Date Night?"

    a. Fifteen-word messages

    b. Newspaper personals

    c. Audio personals

11. According to Susan Block, which are the *best* personals?

    a. The ones with the most information

    b. The ones with nice personalities

    c. The ones with music in the background

12. What does Robert say about himself?

    a. He's thirty-three years old.

    b. He's a passionate eccentric.

    c. He finds women very beautiful.

13. Why doesn't Susan Block like the ads in the paper?

    a. They are too bland.

    b. The information is not true.

    c. The people don't sound attractive.

14. What does she tell people to do when they call in to put ads on her show?

    a. Be themselves.

    b. Be bland.

    c. Be outrageous.

15. What does the woman who calls in say about herself?

    a. She embarrassed somebody she went out with.

    b. She's looking for somebody that's looking for somebody.

    c. Her name is Amy.

LOOKING AT LANGUAGE Two-word Verbs

Many verbs are composed of two words in English (verb + preposition).
When these two words are combined they usually have a new meaning.

Exercise 1

Listen to the following sentences from the interview. For each example,
focus on the words in italics. Try to guess the meaning of each two-word
verb from the context of the interview. Then write a synonym or definition
for each.

1. "I had a wonderful night tonight, I *had* guests *over*,
   played the piano, I had a lot of fun . . . oh, great."

   _____

2. "And sometimes what I'd do with a call-in show is:
   somebody would call in, say it was Linda, and I would
   make up a personal for Linda."

   _____

3. "And she would express herself and then *get off* the
   air."

   _____

4. "Maybe Bob would *call in* and say, 'Hey, that Linda,
   she sounded great! How can I meet her?' "

   _____

5. "And I would just feel terrible that I couldn't *match
   up* poor Bob and poor Linda, who were two single
   people who needed each other. And I thought, 'I'm
   gonna do a show like this myself. I'm gonna *match*
   people *up* on the air.' And that's how 'Date Night'
   started."

   _____

6. "*Tune in* next week, same time, same station, for
   another Saturday night on 'Date Night.' "

   _____

Now try to match each two-word verb with a synonym or similar expression.

_____1. have over   a. set the radio or TV to a certain station

_____2. make up   b. make a telephone call to a talk show

_____3. get off (the air)   c. invite to one's home

_____4. call in   d. write; create

_____5. match up   e. put two people or things together

_____6. tune in   f. stop talking (on radio or TV)

Exercise 2

Some two-word verbs in English are separable; the verb and preposition can be separated by an object. For example:

"I'm gonna *match* people *up* on the air."

In a sentence with a separable two-word verb, the direct object can come between the verb and preposition, or it can come after the verb and preposition:

"I'm gonna *match up* people."

However, if a pronoun is the direct object of the sentence, it must come between the verb and preposition; it cannot come after.

"I'm gonna *match* them *up*."

Read the following sentences. Each two-word verb is an example of a separable two-word verb. Rewrite the sentences using pronouns as direct objects. The first one has been done for you.

    1. Some people don't want to *give up* their freedom just to have a steady boyfriend or girlfriend.

Some people don't want to give it up just to have a steady boyfriend or girlfriend.

2. In the United States, many people go out in cars. It is common for a man to *pick up* his date at her place.

_____

3. People who are engaged to be married sometimes *call off* their engagement just before the wedding.

_____

4. Some women would like to ask men out for a date, but it's hard for them to pick up the phone and *call up* single men.

_____

5. Some women will go out with a man they've never met before; but it's better to *check out* a man before going on the first date.

_____

8 FOLLOW-UP ACTIVITIES

Discussion Questions

In groups, discuss your answers to the following questions.

1. Would you call in to the radio show "Date Night" to meet somebody? Why or why not?
2. Susan Block said that some typical questions asked on "Date Night" were: "What kind of work do you do?," "What movies have you seen?," and "Do you like Chinese food?" What questions would you ask a person when you first meet?

Essay Topics

Choose one of the following topics.

1. Today people often talk about how difficult it is to meet someone of the opposite sex. Do you think that it's more difficult than it was in the past? Why or why not? Write an essay in which you express your opinions.

2. Read the following personal ad, which was presented in the interview:

> Hi. I'm Robert, and I'm forty-three years old, six feet tall, 165 pounds, and I'm in excellent L.A. condition. I'm a passionate eccentric, and I am definitely an acquired taste. Some women have found me very beautiful.

Write your own personal ad for "Date Night." Mention that part of you that is special.

Values Clarification   Dating

Work in groups. Discuss what you look for in a person and why. Read the following criteria that are typically expressed by people who are looking for a date.

Each person in your group should rank these criteria in the order of "most important" (#1) to "least important" (#6). What other criterion would you include? Add it to the list. Compare your ranking with the others' in your group and try to agree on the ranking.

EDUCATION

> The person should be well educated. He or she should be intelligent. The person should have gone to good schools and should have a broad understanding of the world.

GOOD LOOKS

> The person should be attractive. Dress and appearance are very important.

HUMOR

> The person should know how to laugh at life. Being able to joke about things is important.

PERSONALITY

> The person should be very social and be able to get along with many different types of people. He or she should like to go to parties and meet new people.

WEALTH

> The person should have a lot of money. Money is important in today's world, so it is important to be with someone who can afford to pay for nice things, go on trips, etc.

OTHER:

"Meet You on the Air" was first broadcast on *All Things Considered*, April 16, 1986. The interviewer is Wendy Kaufman.

THERE ARE WORSE THINGS THAN DYING

Dr.
Gaes
Offis
For
Kids
With
Cansur

---

1 PREDICTING

From the title, discuss what you think the interview is about.

2 THINK AHEAD

Work in groups. Read the following statements. Do you agree with them? See if everyone in your group has the same opinion.

1. Being sick can sometimes be fun.
2. Children cannot accept death and dying as well as adults can.
3. When you are sad, it's best to talk to someone who is the same age as you.
4. When you do not feel happy, it's OK to cry.

3 VOCABULARY

The words in italics will help you understand the interview. Read the following sentences. Try to guess the meaning of these words from the context of the sentences. Then write a synonym or your own definition of the words.

1. Smoking is one of the leading causes of *cancer*. Every year many people die from this disease.

_____

2. When you are sick and don't know what's wrong, it's best to see a doctor. The doctor can usually *diagnose* the illness.

_____

3. *Radiation treatment* is the most common treatment for cancer patients. It can sometimes stop the disease because the radiation attacks the cancer in the body and destroys it.

_____

4. The bones of the human body are not completely solid; the center of bones is filled with a soft *bone marrow*.

_____

5. A *spinal* is a very painful operation because it removes fluid from the bones.

_____

6. Dogs and cats usually sleep *curled up;* they don't lie straight like people do.

_____

7. People deal with the idea of death and dying differently. Some people feel *apprehensive* about death and don't even want to think about it; others are not afraid of death and accept it as a natural part of the life process.

_____

8. A person who has always lived a healthy and normal life may be *stunned* one day to find out that he or she is dying of a disease. People rarely expect this to happen to them.

_____

9. Some religions teach people that if they are good they will go to *heaven* after they die.

_____

10. Advances in medicine have helped *cure* many people of diseases; years ago, these people would have died from the diseases.

_____

11. Not every treatment will cure a patient of his disease. Even after a long period of feeling well, the patient could experience a *relapse* and become sick again.

_____

Now try to match the words with a definition or synonym. Then compare your answers with those of another student. The first one has been done for you.

_f_ 1. cancer   a. identify an illness

_____ 2. diagnose   b. suffering from an illness again

_____ 3. radiation treatment   c. fearful; scared

_____ 4. bone marrow   d. shocked

_____ 5. spinal   e. material inside the bones

_____ 6. curled up   f. a serious disease

_____ 7. apprehensive   g. place some people believe we go to after death

_____ 8. stunned   h. make healthy

_____ 9. heaven   i. a way to help cancer patients get better

_____ 10. cure   j. operation to remove fluid from the backbone

_____ 11. relapse   k. putting the body in the form of a ball

 4 TASK LISTENING

Listen to the interview. Find the answer to the following question.

Is Jason Gaes cured of cancer?

5 LISTENING FOR MAIN IDEAS

Listen to the interview again. The interview has been divided into four parts. You will hear a beep at the end of each part. Choose the answer that best expresses the main idea in that part. Compare your answers with those of another student.

PART 1 What's the name of Jason's book?

    a. *A book about kids with cancer*
    b. *A book about my cancer*
    c. *My book for kids with cancer*

PART 2 Why did Jason write the book?

    a. He wanted kids to prepare for his death.
    b. He wanted to write a story with a happy ending.
    c. He wanted to talk about the fun things in having cancer.

PART 3 How does Jason's mother explain his reaction to treatment?

    a. He was afraid of dying.
    b. He wasn't afraid of dying.
    c. He was sure he would never die.

PART 4 How have children reacted to Jason's book?

    a. They have decided to get treatment.
    b. They have felt sick to their stomach.
    c. They have called to talk about their cancer.

6 LISTENING FOR DETAILS

Read the questions for Part 1. Then listen to Part 1 again. As you listen, circle the best answer. Compare your answers with those of another student. If you disagree, listen to Part 1 again.

PART 1

1. Where does Jason live?

    a. In Omaha, Nebraska

    b. In Washington

    c. In Minnesota

2. How old was he when he was diagnosed with cancer?

    a. Eight years old

    b. Nine years old

    c. Six years old

3. Which of the procedures does Jason describe in his book?

    a. They give you a shot.

    b. They make you move a lot.

    c. They put "Xs" on your head.

Repeat the same procedure for Parts 2, 3, and 4.

PART 2

4. Who drew the pictures in Jason's book?

    a. His brother Adam

    b. His two brothers

    c. Jason

5. Why didn't Jason like the book *Hang Tough?*

   a. Because the boy in the story went through the same things as Jason

   b. Because the boy in the story died

   c. Because the book wasn't interesting

6. What's fun about having cancer for Jason?

   a. You can have lots of parties.

   b. You get lots of presents.

   c. You can do anything you want to do.

7. Which part of the treatment was the most painful for Jason?

   a. The bone marrow

   b. The spinal tap

   c. The leg pains

PART 3

8. How did Jason want to be treated, according to his mother?

   a. Like a sick child

   b. Like a needy child

   c. Like a normal child

9. Why did Jason say "there are worse things than dying"?

   a. He found out he had cancer.

   b. He didn't want any more painful treatments.

   c. He needed a good ending for his book.

10. How does Jason's mother explain his attitude towards death and dying?

    a. He compares it to being born.

    b. He thinks it's difficult to get to heaven.

    c. He was very afraid of death and dying.

PART 4

11. What advice does Jason give to kids?

   a. Don't be scared.

   b. Talk to your mom.

   c. Don't cry.

12. What did Jason tell the little girl who called him?

   a. She would feel a little pain.

   b. She would feel dry and sick.

   c. The operation would work.

13. What last advice does Jason give kids who have cancer?

   a. Never forget that they have cancer.

   b. Try to live a normal life.

   c. Get many treatments.

7 LOOKING AT LANGUAGE Idioms

Several idioms were used in the interview with Jason. Read the following statements as you listen to the tape. Try to determine the meaning of the italicized idioms in these sentences. Write a synonym or your own definition of each one. Then compare your answers with those of another student.

1. Jason:
   "One time I came home with a book, and it was called *Hang Tough*, and I thought *it was really neat* because that boy was going through the same things as I was going through."

   _____

2. Jason:
   "One time I came home with a book, and it was called *Hang Tough*, and I thought it was really neat because that boy *was going through* the same things as I was going through."

   _____

3. Jason:
    "And the last two or three pages it told about . . . he died . . . and
    it stunk."
    Interviewer:
    "It stunk?"
    Jason:
    "Uh-huh."
    Interviewer:
    "Cause he died?"
    Jason:
    "Uh-huh."

    _____

4. Interviewer:
    "In one page you write that having cancer isn't fun."
    Jason:
    "*It ain't no party.*"

    _____

5. Interviewer:
    "Mrs. Gaes, Jason, in his book, writes about some bad moments.
    How did he hold up?"
    Mrs. Gaes:
    "For the most part, very, very well. Jason insisted on not being
    treated as a sick child."

    _____

6. Interviewer:
    "Jason, you wrote this book because you said you were *tired of*
    reading books about kids who had cancer and who died in the end.
    Was there any time, during all this treatment, when you thought
    maybe dying wouldn't be so bad?"

    _____

7. Jason:
    "When *it was all over with.*"

    _____

8. Interviewer:
    "Jason, have kids called you?"
    Jason:
    "Yeah. *You bet!* Lots of kids have called me."

    _____

Now try to match the idioms with another phrase or expression that has similar meaning.

_____1. It was really neat!

_____2. He was going through something.

_____3. It stunk.

_____4. It ain't no party.

_____5. How did he hold up?

_____6. He was tired of it.

_____7. It was all over with.

_____8. You bet!

a. How did he manage?

b. It was finished.

c. It was terrible.

d. It was great!

e. Yes, of course.

f. It isn't fun.

g. He was experiencing something.

h. He had too much of it.

8 FOLLOW-UP ACTIVITIES

Discussion Questions

In groups, discuss your answers to the following questions.

1. Imagine that Jason Gaes had decided not to continue his treatments. Should a person suffering from a fatal disease be allowed to end his or her life? Should a doctor assist a patient in ending his or her life?

2. Would a book written by a child have more of an effect on another child than a book written by an adult? Why or why not?

Essay Topics

Choose one of the following topics.

1. Jason said there were worse things than dying. He wasn't afraid of dying because his treatments were so painful. For him, the pain of the treatments was worse than his fear of death.

   How do people in your culture deal with death and dying? Write an essay in which you describe this cultural attitude.

2. Jason wrote a book to help kids with cancer. Have you ever wanted to help people because of something you were going through? Write an essay in which you describe your experience.

Role-play Death and Dying

For this role-play, the class is divided into four groups. One group will prepare Miriam's arguments. Another group will prepare the arguments of Miriam's sister. Another group will prepare the arguments of Miriam's son. And the final group will prepare the arguments of the doctor. Read the situation, choose a group, and after a twenty-minute preparation, begin the discussion.

THE SITUATION

Miriam is sixty-six years old. She has lived alone since her husband died several years ago. Her sister lives near her and visits her regularly. Although she does not work, she leads a very active life. She is a member of the local Town Planning Council and is an active member of her church.

Six months ago, however, Miriam was diagnosed as having cancer. She has become very sick over the past few months. The doctor has been treating her with chemotherapy—a treatment which uses chemicals to stop the spread of cancer. The doctors say that she might be cured with this treatment. But there are no guarantees, and many patients experience a relapse of cancer after treatment.

The problem is that the treatment has made Miriam very sick. Each time she goes to the hospital, she becomes very apprehensive because she knows that she will get sick to her stomach. Since she started receiving treatment, she has become very depressed.

This week Miriam made a decision. She decided to stop the chemotherapy. She says that she would prefer to let nature take its course rather than to suffer anymore. Miriam's son, Jack, lives with his own family in another part of the country. When he heard her decision, he became very upset. He decided to go and see his mother; he wants to convince her not to stop the treatment. The doctors have tried to convince her to continue the treatment, too. But Miriam says that she has made her decision. Tomorrow, Miriam's son is coming to see her. Miriam's sister, Emily, is also coming. They will all discuss Miriam's treatment with the doctor.

THE ROLES

MIRIAM

> You are very sick from the chemotherapy. It is more painful than you had ever expected. You realize that your life will never be the same with cancer. You have lived a full life. You don't want to continue the treatment. For you, it's worse than dying.

EMILY

> You have lived near Miriam for most of your life. You understand Miriam's suffering and feel she should be able to make her own decision about the chemotherapy. Your sister was always very active. You have watched her get more and more depressed. You support her decision to stop the treatment.

JACK

> You think your mother is not being rational. You tell her to think of what will happen if she stops the chemotherapy. You believe the treatment can work. You want to convince your mother to continue.

DR. KIRK

> You have treated cancer patients for fifteen years. Some of those patients are still living today because of chemotherapy. You realize that Miriam is experiencing a lot of pain, but you want her to understand that chemotherapy is the only way her cancer may be cured.

PROCEDURE FOR DISCUSSION

1. Form new groups to include at least one person playing each of the roles. Miriam, Emily, and Jack meet with Dr. Kirk. Each person presents his or her point of view to Miriam.
2. Miriam listens and reacts to their opinions. Miriam's sister and son try to convince each other of their opinions.
3. After a fifteen- to twenty-minute discussion, Miriam decides what she will do.
4. The group then compares Miriam's decision with the decision of the other groups in class.

"There Are Worse Things than Dying" was first broadcast on *All Things Considered*, September 16, 1987. The interviewer is Renee Montaigne.

A COUCH POTATO

1 **PREDICTING**

From the title, discuss what you think the interview is about.

2 THINK AHEAD

In groups, discuss your answers to the following questions.

1. In your opinion, what is the best way to relax? Do you prefer watching TV, reading a book or magazine, or some other form of relaxation?
2. Do you spend time with your family during the holidays? What do you do together? Do you spend any of this time watching television as a family?
3. How much TV do you watch a week? Would you rather watch more or less? Why?

3 VOCABULARY

The following words will help you understand the interview. Try to guess the meaning of the words. Use your knowledge of English, or use your dictionaries. In each set of words, cross out the word that does not have a similar meaning to the italicized word. Then compare your answers with those of another student. Discuss why these words are similar. The first one has been done for you.

1. *coin a phrase*	develop a name	create a term	~~print~~ ~~money~~
2. *junk food*	soda	potato chips	~~oatmeal~~
3. *head*	founder	~~secretary~~	president
4. *tolerate*	accept	endure	~~abandon~~
5. *hearth*	~~workplace~~	home	fireplace
6. *guilt*	wrong doing	~~pride~~	shame
7. *tuber*	potato	underground root	~~disease~~
8. *icon*	~~ice~~	symbol	picture
9. *tube*	television	TV	~~telephone~~
10. *physique*	shape	build	~~chemistry~~
11. *ballast*	stability	weight	~~quality~~

4   TASK LISTENING

Listen to the interview. Find the answer to the following question.

> What is an important time for couch potatoes?

holidays

5   LISTENING FOR MAIN IDEAS

Listen to the interview again. The interview has been divided into four parts. You will hear a beep at the end of each part. As you listen, circle the answer that best expresses the main idea in that part. Compare your answers with those of another student.

PART 1   What did Robert Armstrong do?

     a. He founded a club for people who like to watch TV.
     b. He started a club for cartoonists.
     c. He created a T-shirt company.

PART 2   Why are the holidays important for couch potatoes?

     a. Families go to football games together.
     b. Families turn off the TV.
     c. Families spend time together.

PART 3   Why is there a need for a club like the Couch Potatoes?

     a. People suffer from watching TV.
     b. People eat too many potatoes.
     c. People feel guilty about how much TV they watch.

PART 4   What kinds of TV program do couch potatoes watch?

     a. Only the most popular TV shows
     b. Programs on member stations
     c. Anything on TV

6 LISTENING FOR DETAILS

Read the statements for Part 1. Then listen to Part 1 again and decide whether the statements are true or false. As you listen, write a *T* or *F* next to each statement. Compare your answers with those of another student. If you disagree, listen to Part 1 again.

PART 1

_T_ 1. Robert Armstrong lives in California.

_F_ 2. He coined the phrase "couch potato" in 1966.

_F_ 3. The phrase seems old to the interviewer.

_F_ 4. There are 8,500 couch potato clubs.

_T_ 5. Members receive handbooks, newsletters, and T-shirts.

Repeat the same procedure for Parts 2, 3, and 4.

PART 2

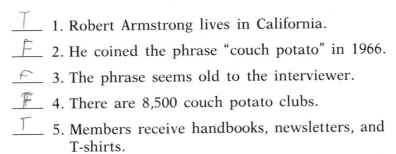

According to Robert Armstrong . . .

_F_ 6. Men and women watch football games on TV during the holidays.

_T_ 7. Families get along better if they watch TV.

_F_ 8. Family members can never agree on a TV program to watch.

PART 3

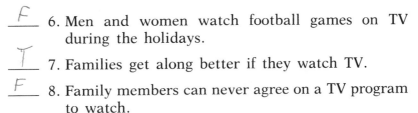

_F_ 9. Most people agree that watching TV is an intellectual activity.

_T_ 10. Some people lie about how much TV they watch.

_F_ 11. Robert Armstrong thinks couch potatoes should put their TVs in the closet.

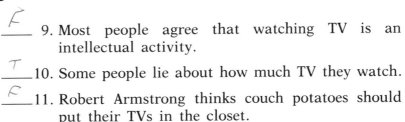

_T_ 12. The potato is the icon for couch potatoes.

_T_ 13. Some couch potatoes get a potato shape from watching so much TV.

_F_ 14. Robert Armstrong says couch potatoes roll off the couch easily.

PART 4

_T_ 15. "Love Boat" is one of the favorite TV shows of couch potatoes.

_T_ 16. Couch potatoes think that "if it's on TV, it must be good."

7 LOOKING AT LANGUAGE Puns

Exercise 1

In this interview, Robert Armstrong explains the origin of the name "couch potato." He makes two puns in his explanation. A pun is a play on words to make people laugh. It is formed by using words that sound alike or words that have more than one meaning. Read the two examples of puns:

Type A—Words that Sound Alike

Example:	"What is black and white and *red* all over?"
Answer:	"A newspaper."
Explanation:	"Red" is the same sound as "read," the past participle of "to read."

Type B—Words that Have More than One Meaning

Example:	"What has four wheels and *flies*?"
Answer:	"A garbage truck."
Explanation:	"Flies" can mean "goes through the air" (verb), or it can mean "insects" (noun).

Listen to this segment of the interview. Then discuss the two puns with a partner.

Armstrong:

> We, as couch potatoes, beckon people to "come out of the closet," and claim it loud that they are a tuber and proud. The "tuber" part of it is one of the reasons why we selected the potato to be our icon, because it is, after all, *a tuber* and has many *eyes*."

Interviewer:

> Oh, I just got it! As in "tube."

Armstrong:

> Yes, watching the tube, and all the eyes of the potato used to watch TV with. It just seemed like a good symbol for us to rally around.

Explanation

Robert Armstrong is making a pun when he talks about a *tuber* with many *eyes*. This is a Type B pun. He is playing with the two meanings of these words:

1) The potato comes from the *tuber* family (a type of underground root). Television is frequently called "the *tube*" because it has an electronic tube inside. Therefore, a person who watches TV is humorously called "a *tuber*."
2) The potato has *eyes* (marks on the potato which are called "eyes") and we use our *eyes* to watch TV.

Exercise 2

Puns are often used in jokes. Work with another student. Discuss the three choices for each joke. Choose the answer which makes a pun and try to explain the play on words. Then decide whether it is an example of a Type A or Type B pun. The first one has been done for you.

Type

___B___ 1. What did the mayonnaise say to the refrigerator?

        a. It's too cold in here! I'm freezing.
        (b.) Close the door! I'm dressing.
        c. Let me out! It's time to eat.

Explanation: "Dressing" has two meanings: 1) putting clothes on (verb) and 2) a sauce which is put on salad (noun). This is a Type B pun.

_____ 2. Why is a baseball team like a good pancake?

        (a.) It has to have a good batter.
        b. They both run a lot.
        c. It has to have good players.

_____ 3. My doctor put me on a seafood diet, and now I only eat when . . .

        a. I can have lobster.
        (b.) I see food.
        c. I go fishing.

_____ 4. Why are chefs mean?

        a. Because they heat the butter and stir the sauce.
        b. Because they beat the eggs and whip the cream.
        c. Because they grease the pans and bake the bread.

_____ 5. How do you know that robbers are really strong?

    a. They lift weights.
    b. They break into safes.
    c. They hold up banks.

_____ 6. What did the ocean say to the shore?

    a. Nothing, it just waved.
    b. It asked it to move closer.
    c. It told it to stay dry.

_____ 7. What is a protein?

    a. A chemical substitute for meat.
    b. Someone interested in sports.
    c. Someone in favor of teenagers.

_____ 8. Why was the baseball player arrested?

    a. Because they found him drinking at home.
    b. Because they caught him stealing bases.
    c. Because they found him throwing things.

_____ 9. Why does John always wear a wristwatch?

    a. He likes to take his time.
    b. He has a busy schedule.
    c. He doesn't want to lose it.

_____ 10. What are the strongest days?

    a. Monday and Tuesday. They're after the weekend.
    b. Saturday and Sunday. All the rest are weekdays.
    c. Wednesday and Thursday. They fall in the middle.

Exercise 3

Puns are also used in advertising. Look at each ad. Try to explain the pun. Then determine what type of pun it is.

ITS POWER WILL MOVE YOU.
ITS BEAUTY WILL STOP YOU.
The new Jergen sports coupe.

Word processing anybody can pick up.

Hanson's portable word processor

Schneider's Jewellers

Carats are great for your eyes.

8 FOLLOW-UP ACTIVITIES

Discussion Questions

In groups, discuss your answers to the following questions.

1. Do you agree with Robert Armstrong, that watching TV helps "keep the peace" among family members? Does your family have difficulty deciding what to watch on

TV? How does your family decide what to watch?

2. Do you agree that "if it's on TV, it must be good"? Do you agree that most TV programming is good? In your opinion, are there any shows that should *not* be on television? Or, would you censor any programs in your own home? If so, which ones?

Essay Topics

Choose one of the following topics.

1. Write a letter to the "Couch Potato" newsletter. Tell the readers of the newsletter what you think of their club and the idea of couch potatoes.
2. Do you suffer from "intellectual guilt" about how much TV you watch? Write an essay in which you express your feelings about the quantity and quality of TV that you watch.

Debate How Much TV?

For this debate, the class is divided into two teams. The debate will focus on whether or not TV viewing should be limited.

Team A will argue in favor of unlimited TV viewing.

> You believe that people should watch as much TV as they like. You will argue that people get a lot of important information from television and that watching TV is a good form of relaxation. You also think that TV is the quickest way to find out what is happening in today's busy world.

Team B will argue in favor of limiting TV viewing.

> You believe that people should limit their TV viewing to one hour a day. You will argue that television creates unnecessary desires. You think that TV teaches values that are not good. You also think TV creates passivity in people.

Prepare your arguments. A moderator will lead the debate.

Debate Procedures

Team A begins with a three-minute presentation.
Team B then gives a three-minute presentation.
Team A responds to Team B's presentation for three minutes.
Team B responds to Team A's presentation for three minutes.

After the debate, the moderator evaluates the strength of both arguments.

"A Couch Potato" was first broadcast on *Morning Edition*, December 27, 1987. The interviewer is Susan Stamberg.

ANSWER KEY

UNIT 1   THE LAST INNOCENT MEAL

3. VOCABULARY

1. old-fashioned 2. focused 3. depressing
4. mixtures 5. supermarkets 6. fruit 7. solid
8. remain 9. attracted to 10. smooth 11. thick

4. TASK LISTENING

Oatmeal.

5. LISTENING FOR MAIN IDEAS

Part 1:b, Part 2:c, Part 3:b

6. LISTENING FOR DETAILS

Part 1:   1. T 2. F 3. F 4. F 5. T 6. T 7. F
Part 2:   8. T 9. F 10. F 11. T 12. T 13. T
          14. F 15. F
Part 3:   16. T 17. T 18. F 19. T 20. F 21. T

7. LOOKING AT LANGUAGE

Exercise 1
1. pour 2. stir 3. cover 4. let stand 5. heat
6. stir 7. serve

Exercise 2

COMBINING INGREDIENTS	CHANGING THE CONSISTENCY OF FOOD	PREPARING TO COOK	COOKING FOOD	GETTING READY TO EAT
pour	let stand	cover	heat	serve
stir	sift	preheat	bake	
add	cream	grease		
beat	———			
combine	beat			
mix				
blend				
measure				
sift				
cream				

UNIT 2   LIVING THROUGH DIVORCE

3. VOCABULARY

1. b 2. h 3. g 4. i 5. a 6. d 7. f 8. e 9. c 10. j

4. TASK LISTENING

Her parents are getting divorced.

5. LISTENING FOR MAIN IDEAS

Part 1:c, Part 2:b, Part 3:c

6. LISTENING FOR DETAILS

Part 1:   1. F 2. T 3. T 4. T 5. T 6. F 7. F 8. F
          9. F
Part 2:   10. F 11. T 12. T 13. F 14. F 15. F
          16. T 17. T 18. F
Part 3:   19. T 20. T 21. F 22. F 23. F 24. T

7. LOOKING AT LANGUAGE

Exercise 1
The sender's address
The date
The salutation
The body
Special greeting
The close
The signature

Exercise 2

FORMAL EXPRESSIONS	INFORMAL EXPRESSIONS
Dear Mr. McCarthy:	Dear Eric,
Dear Sir:	Take care.
To whom it may concern:	Write soon.
All the best.	Love,
I look forward to hearing	Fondly,
from you.	
Sincerely,	
Yours truly,	

UNIT 3   A BOY'S SHELTER FOR STREET PEOPLE

3. VOCABULARY

1. wealthy people 2. calming 3. relented
4. wise 5. salary 6. charge 7. comprehension
8. politically 9. caring 10. religion

4. TASK LISTENING

His father, Frank Ferrell.

5. LISTENING FOR MAIN IDEAS

Part 1:c, Part 2:b, Part 3:a, Part 4:b

6. LISTENING FOR DETAILS

Part 1:   1. a 2. c 3. a 4. a 5. b
Part 2:   6. c 7. c 8. b 9. a 10. b 11. c
Part 3:   12. a 13. b 14. a 15. a
Part 4:   16. b 17. a 18. b 19.b

7. LOOKING AT LANGUAGE

Exercise 2
1. Food is donated to the homeless by fast
   food chains.
2. Free food is given to the homeless by
   volunteers.
3. The homeless were helped by Trevor.
4. Trevor was interviewed by a journalist.
5. The shelter was named "Trevor's Place" by
   the homeless people.

Exercise 3
1. put 2. was interviewed 3. was published
4. sent 5. was donated 6. volunteered
7. contributed 8. started 9. was opened
10. was named

UNIT 4   WHERE THE GIRLS AND BOYS ARE

3. VOCABULARY

7, 8, 1, 5, 2, 6, 3, 4, 9

5. LISTENING FOR MAIN IDEAS

Part 1:c, Part 2:a, Part 3:b

6. LISTENING FOR DETAILS

Part 1:   1. c 2. c
Part 2:   3. a 4. a 5. c 6. b
Part 3:   7. c 8. c 9. c 10. b

7. LOOKING AT LANGUAGE

Exercise 1
1. male 2. Fish 3. mate 4. so 5. are 6. she
7. longing 8. sex 9. fowl 10. should 11. every
12. boys 13. she 14. Where 15. place

Exercise 2
1. more interesting than 2. more than
3. larger than 4. greater than 5. higher than
6. more than 7. fewer than 8. more
concentrated 9. warmer than 10. more
populated 11. more than

UNIT 5   THE THINKING CAP

3. VOCABULARY

1. e 2. j 3. f 4. d 5. h 6. c 7. i 8. k 9. a 10. g
11. b

4. TASK LISTENING

It warms it.

5. LISTENING FOR MAIN IDEAS

Part 1:c, Part 2:c, Part 3:a, Part 4:a

6. LISTENING FOR DETAILS

Part 1:   1. T 2. T 3. F 4. F
Part 2:   5. F 6. F 7. F 8. T 9. T
Part 3:   10. T 11. F 12. F 13. T 14. T
Part 4:   15. F 16. F 17. F 18. F 19. T 20. F

7. LOOKING AT LANGUAGE

Exercise 2
1. needed, would put on
2. had to, would wear
3. would use, wanted
4. raised, would increase
5. sold, would buy

UNIT 6   WHO IS MORE AFRAID OF
NUCLEAR WAR?

3. VOCABULARY

8, 9, 4, 2, 3, 5, 6, 7, 10, 1

4. TASK LISTENING

The United States and the Soviet Union.

5. LISTENING FOR MAIN IDEAS

Part 1:a, Part 2:c, Part 3:a, Part 4:b, Part 5:b

6. LISTENING FOR DETAILS

Part 1:   1. T 2. T 3. F 4. F 5. T 6. T
Part 2:   7. F 8. T
Part 3:   9. T 10. T
Part 4:   11. T 12. F 13. T 14. F 15. F 16. T
Part 5:   17. T 18. T 19. T 20. F

7. LOOKING AT LANGUAGE

Exercise 2

1. He said that he thought a nuclear war was very likely.
2. They said that they thought their leaders would never let it happen.
3. She said that she didn't believe anyone could survive a nuclear war.
4. They said that they didn't think it was possible to survive a nuclear war.
5. She said that retaliation was the only way to deal with an attack.
6. They said that they thought retaliation was probably necessary.
7. He said that he thought life would be better for his children.
8. They said that their children's lives would probably not be as good as their lives.

UNIT 7   AT THE TABLE

3. VOCABULARY

1. c 2. i 3. k 4. a 5. h 6. e 7. d 8. g 9. f 10. b
11. j

4. TASK LISTENING

dirty fingernails, brushing teeth, candles on the table, flowers on the table, wine service

5. LISTENING FOR MAIN IDEAS

Part 1:c, Part 2:c, Part 3:b

6. LISTENING FOR DETAILS

Part 1:   1. F 2. T 3. T
Part 2:   4. T 5. T 6. F 7. F 8. T
Part 3:   9. F 10. T 11. T 12. F 13. F 14. T

UNIT 8   FROM ONE WORLD TO ANOTHER

3. VOCABULARY

1. poll 2. ignore 3. study 4. produce 5. house
6. separate from 7. joined 8. glance at
9. neglect 10. creation

4. TASK LISTENING

She is a native American Indian (Oneida & Mohawk).

5. LISTENING FOR MAIN IDEAS

Part 1:b, Part 2:a, Part 3:c, Part 4:a

6. LISTENING FOR DETAILS

Part 1:   1. a 2. b 3. a 4. b
Part 2:   5. a 6. c 7. c
Part 3:   8. c 9. c 10. c
Part 4:   11. a 12. a 13. b

7. LOOKING AT LANGUAGE

Exercise 1

1. high 2. Smoke 3. promise 4. air 5. brush
6. west 7. melting 8. know 9. snow 10. miles
11. morning 12. feather 13. broken 14. dark
15. air 16. dreams

Exercise 2

ANIMALS & PARTS OF THE BODY OF AN ANIMAL	PLANTS	TIME OF DAY	WEATHER	DESCRIPTIVE VERBS
horses	cedar	moon	breeze	trembling
tails	grasses	darkness	snow	glow
crickets		morning		lumbers
ice bear				gleams
feather				melting
gull				brush
down				breathe
				dying

UNIT 9   TO FINISH FIRST

3. VOCABULARY

4, 5, 6, 3, 9, 2, 10, 7, 8, 1

4. TASK LISTENING

No.

5. LISTENING FOR MAIN IDEAS

Part 1:a, Part 2:a, Part 3:a, Part 4:b, Part 5:c

6. LISTENING FOR DETAILS

Part 1:   1. T 2. F 3. T 4. T 5. T
Part 2:   6. T 7. T 8. T 9. T 10. T 11. F
Part 3:   12. F 13. T 14. T 15. F
Part 4:   16. $3,200 17. $40,000 18. 1 day
          19. 1 hour 20. 5–6 hours 21. 4 hours
Part 5:   22. 1 year 23. 20 teams 24. 10 years
          25. 1925

7. LOOKING AT LANGUAGE

Exercise 2

1. a two-week race 2. a ten-day race 3. a four-hour rest 4. a thirty-two hundred dollar prize 5. a forty-thousand dollar training 6. a fourteen-member dog team 7. an eight-hour detour

UNIT 10   MEET YOU ON THE AIR

3. VOCABULARY

1. place 2. married 3. long discussion 4. wife 5. destroy 6. argument 7. cold 8. average 9. outrageous

4. TASK LISTENING

playing the piano, going to the beach, eating Chinese food

5. LISTENING FOR MAIN IDEAS

Part 1:a, Part 2:b, Part 3:a, Part 4:c

6. LISTENING FOR DETAILS

Part 1:   1. c 2. b 3. c 4. c
Part 2:   5. a 6. a
Part 3:   7. a 8. c 9. c
Part 4:   10. c 11. c 12. b 13. a 14. a 15. b

7. LOOKING AT LANGUAGE

Exercise 1
1. c 2. d 3. f 4. b 5. e 6. a

Exercise 2
1. Some people don't want to give it up just to have a steady boyfriend or girlfriend.
2. It is common for a man to pick her up at her place.
3. People who are engaged to be married sometimes call it off just before the wedding.
4. Some women would like to ask men out for a date, but it's hard for them to pick up the phone and call them up.
5. But it's better to check him out before going on the first date.

UNIT 11   THERE ARE WORSE THINGS THAN DYING

3. VOCABULARY

1. f 2. a 3. i 4. e 5. j 6. k 7. c 8. d 9. g 10. h 11. b

4. TASK LISTENING

Yes.

5. LISTENING FOR MAIN IDEAS

Part 1:c, Part 2:b, Part 3:b, Part 4:c

6. LISTENING FOR DETAILS

Part 1:   1. c 2. c 3. c
Part 2:   4. b 5. b 6. b 7. a
Part 3:   8. c 9. b 10. a
Part 4:   11. b 12. b 13. b

7. LOOKING AT LANGUAGE

Exercise 1
1. d 2. g 3. c 4. f 5. a 6. h 7. b 8. e

UNIT 12   A COUCH POTATO

3. VOCABULARY

1. print money 2. oatmeal 3. secretary 4. abandon 5. workplace 6. pride 7. disease 8. ice 9. telephone 10. chemistry 11. quality

4. TASK LISTENING

The holidays.

5. LISTENING FOR MAIN IDEAS

Part 1:a, Part 2:c, Part 3:c, Part 4:c

6. LISTENING FOR DETAILS

Part 1:   1. T 2. F 3. F 4. F 5. T
Part 2:   6. F 7. T 8. F
Part 3:   9. F 10. T 11. F 12. T 13. T 14. F
Part 4:   15. T 16. T

7. LOOKING AT LANGUAGE
Exercise 1
1. Type B, b
2. Type B, a
3. Type A, b
4. Type B, b
5. Type B, c
6. Type B, a
7. Type A, c
8. Type B, b
9. Type B, a
10. Type A, b

TAPESCRIPT

UNIT 1:   The Last Innocent Meal

Introduction: Marian Cunningham believes that breakfast is the last innocent meal, and it is for that reason that the food columnist for the *San Francisco Chronicle* has done a new book called *The Breakfast Book*, out these days, just about any moment, from Knopf. You say it's the last innocent meal, Marian, which means what? It's not trendy, it's not chic?

Cunningham: That's quite right. It's simple. It is old-fashioned, or rather than old-fashioned, there's something timeless about breakfast. I just have thought that it was overlooked. There's so many very good brunch books out, but that's such a different meal.

Stamberg: Breakfast is not the same as brunch, is it?

Cunningham: It's not the same at all. Brunch is really a festive affair, and very often there're wines, and all kinds of beverages are served that are more celebratory. Breakfast isn't that way. Breakfast is very personal. To me, it also has very limited ingredients, at least my definition, which are grains, dairy products, fruits and eggs, perhaps, or a little meat and fish, and that's just about it.

Stamberg: Mm-hm.

Cunningham: That's the way I think of breakfast.

Stamberg: Basic farm ingredients, not things that you have to go to four gourmet shops in order to gather, huh?

Cunningham: That's exactly right, Susan. Simple, but simple can be so very good, and I think we forget it sometimes.

Stamberg: Give us an example of just plain, simple, good breakfast food.

Cunningham: Well, I think that this would be a wonderful surprise to lots of people . . . the use of rolled oats. And this comes really from Scotland and Ireland. It's called "Irish oatmeal" sometimes, although it is, these are rolled oats, and not the steel-cut oats. But simply taking, let's say, a cup or maybe only ⅔ cup of oats and pour 1½ cups of boiling water over it, with a little salt in the water. Stir it, cover it, and let it stand overnight, preferably in a very low oven, 200 degrees, all night long. In the morning, I simply heat it as hot as I wish, and stir and serve. What happens in that long sitting and resting period is that it becomes very translucent and very oatsy tasting. There's also a nice creaminess. It really transforms what we're accustomed to eating.

Stamberg: Hah!

Cunningham: There's nothing wrong with what we normally eat, but this is wonderfully different.

Stamberg: Are you cooking the oatmeal the night before, or are you just pouring the boiling water . . .

Cunningham: Well, if you can keep it, say, over a very low double boiler, with enough water in it, or even a crock pot or something like that, the oven works very well for me.

Just in a very low oven, and maybe in a pan of hot water, just to keep a little warmth going all night long.

Stamberg: Hmm.

Cunningham: But even so, if you aren't able to do that, and pour boiling water over it, cover it, and just let it sit all night. It's a real discovery . . .

Stamberg: Hah!

Cunningham: And a wonderful one.

Stamberg: Have you any lump theory, Marian Cunningham? I remember at summer camp, the mean jokes people used to tell about lumps in the oatmeal. Do they make oatmeal really horrible, or is it just that it looks awful?
(Both laugh)

Cunningham: It . . . it . . . I think there is a new day look to oatmeal that we're buying. The rolled oats very rarely lump. If they lump, it's because not enough liquid has been added.

Stamberg: Aah!

Cunningham: Not that they should be soupy, by any means. It should have a nice, slightly firm, but soft and creamy texture normally. Lumpiness comes from too much dryness or a rolled oat that is so coarse that it just doesn't soften up in water.

Stamberg: So it's the rolled oat that is lump-proof.

Cunningham: Well, it is. Absolutely, lumps should not exist.

Stamberg: Fantastic. What's your favorite way to serve that nice, piping-hot oatmeal?

Cunningham: Oh, I love it with brown sugar, and a little bit of cream, or light cream. My ideal is to have a piece of toasted pound cake right next to it.

Stamberg: Marian Cunningham. Her new work, *The Breakfast Book*, is just out.

UNIT 2:   Living through Divorce

Noah Adams: Betsy, tell me your full name, please.

Betsy: Betsy Allison Walter.

Adams: Betsy Allison Walter, and you're eight years old?

Betsy: Almost nine.

Adams: And you live in Manhattan?

Betsy: Mm-hm.

Adams: And you're in our studio in New York. I appreciate your taking some time to come in and telling us this story. You wrote a letter to the mayor of New York, Mayor Koch.

Betsy: Right.

Adams: Tell me about that, please.

Betsy: Well, I wrote to him because my parents are getting divorced, and I really don't know who to turn to, and I just told him that my parents are getting divorced, and my dad is with somebody else, and I was just getting used to something, and now this, and it's really kinda hard on me, and I'd like an opinion.

Adams: Why did you write to . . . to Mayor Koch?

Betsy: 'Cause he's somebody who I've thought, he's very good to us, I guess, 'cause he's the mayor, and he knows a lot of things, and I thought he would know about this too.

Adams: Yeah. Did you get an answer back?

Betsy: Yes.

Adams: What'd he say?

Betsy: He, um, it's very short. "Thank you for the letter. I was saddened to learn of the difficult times you are experiencing now. It is important for you to share your feelings and thoughts with someone during this time. I wish there is . . . was an easy solution to these problems, but there is not. Please remember that you are loved and that pe . . . that people care about you. All the best. Sincerely, Edward Koch."

Adams: Mm. Was that reassuring to you, in a way?

Betsy: No.

Adams: No? Did you have any thought in your mind that, perhaps he could actually do something about it? For example, call your father, and get your mom and dad back together?

Betsy: No.

Adams: No, you just wanted some advice.

Betsy: But see, I tried to sometimes, like, 'cause I had a dance recital one day, and I'd invite 'em both, but I wanted them to sit next to each other, but they didn't.

Adams: Yeah. What other advice have you been able to come across? To . . . to find?

Betsy: Well, the guidance counselor, she said that it, a lot of kids have the same problems, say, there're 400 in school, say, and like 300 of them have the same problem.

Adams: Sure—sure. You know, most people you talk with will have had parents who were divorced.

Betsy: Oh.

Adams: Yeah. Most people. It's kind of a sad thing, but most people get through it all right, too. That's my advice for you.

Betsy: Thank you.

Adams: You wrote another letter to somebody who, who had written a book called *The Boys' and Girls' Book of Divorce?*

Betsy: Yes.

Adams: A psychologist?

Betsy: Mm-hm.

Adams: And what did that person tell you?

Betsy: Well, he said that I should try another of his books to find out help.

Adams: Oh, he wanted you to go out and buy his book. Did you?

Betsy: Well, we had the one he recommended.

Adams: And how did that go? What did you think of that one?

Betsy: Well, the problem is, he puts things in a way that I can't really quite get it through me, that I already know, and I want some really, advice that my questions really are—not just answers that people keep telling me over and over again.

Adams: Can you give me an example, Betsy?

Betsy: Why did they get divorced? What happened?

Adams: Do you think that . . . that parents sometimes don't think children are old enough to understand or can't handle it, and so will hide some information?

Betsy: Yes.

Adams: Not that they have to say everything, but you think there ought to be a little bit more sharing of the information.

Betsy: Yeah, my . . . that's what my mom said.

Adams: Yeah. And in terms of their own divorce, do you understand it better now?

Betsy: No.

Adams: No? Why? What still don't you understand about that?

Betsy: Well, why did they have to go off and do it, 'n' 'cause, see, the most painful part is when I saw my Dad packing up, and, and I really don't understand because, like, it's hard to, 'cause they won't tell me what happened to them, and I really want 'em back together and I don't understand why they can't.

Adams: Yeah. What do you think you've learned from this, do you think if . . . if somebody else in school, for example, told you that their parents were getting divorced, how do . . . how do you think you could advise them?

Betsy: Well, I wrote a book, and I said, and I think I would say the same information that I said.

Adams: You wrote a very small book?

Betsy: Yeah.

Adams: Yeah. Do you have it there?

Betsy: Mm-hm.

Adams: Could you read some of it for me, please?

Betsy: All right. Let me get it. It's called *A Book About Divorce*. Should I read the whole book, it's short?

Adams: Sure.

Betsy: "It's not your fault when your parents get divorced. Why does it have to be you? Because Mommy and Daddy don't love each other any more. Remember, it's OK to be sad and cry. Tell someone about your feelings." That's it.

Adams: That's nice. Listen, Betsy, thank you for talking with us. I appreciate it, and I . . . and I wish the best. I hope things go well for you.

Betsy: Thank you.

Adams: And maybe, maybe this is the beginning of a writing experience for you, and you can grow up to be a writer.

Betsy: I don't want to. But I want to write like one book that would make it, but not a whole series, you know.

Adams: You just want to write a book and make a lot of money.

Betsy: No, not money, just famous.

Adams: OK. OK, Betsy, thank you. Good night.

UNIT 3: A Boy's Shelter for Street People

Introduction: It was about two years ago, on a cold night in December, when eleven-year-old Trevor Ferrell first realized that there were people living out on the streets of Philadelphia, just twelve miles from his nice, comfortable suburban home. Trevor saw a news report about the city's homeless. He ran to tell his parents about this startling discovery. Trevor wanted to do something, right away, that night. He wanted his mother and father to take him into the city so he could help someone. His amazed parents resisted the idea at first, but then relented, thinking it would be a good lesson for their impressionable son. They never expected he would want to do it again. They didn't realize what else Trevor would learn that night.

Trevor: I saw a man living on the street, when we got into the city, and I brought in a blanket and a pillow that night, and I gave it to the man, and he looked really comfortable, and said "God bless you," and it made me feel really good.

Neary: It felt so good that Trevor went back the next night, and the next, and the next. Pretty soon, his family ran out of pillows and blankets and old clothes. So they put an ad in a local paper for donations. The paper decided to find out what Trevor and his family were up to, so they interviewed him, and his story was published. Donations poured in; people volunteered to help; someone contributed a van. So they started giving out free food as well. And now, there is a permanent shelter for the homeless in Philadelphia, dubbed Trevor's Place by the people who stay there. Trevor's story is the subject of a book, *Trevor's Place*, written by his parents, Frank and Janet Ferrell. Trevor's initial act of kindness has become a full-time commitment, and Trevor has become close friends with many of the people he met on the streets.

Trevor: There's Chico, Ralph, um . . . Big Joe . . . there's a lot.

Neary: Well, who are the street people? What's their background? How did they get to be living in the street?

Trevor: Well, some of them lost their jobs, some of them, um, have mental problems, some of them drink, and all it takes is for yuh, for somebody to be out in the streets for two or three days, and then you start looking dirty, and it's . . . it's really hard. My Dad and I tried staying on the street one night, and we couldn't even try—we couldn't take it; we had to leave.

Neary: How . . . how long did you . . . how long did you try it, Frank?

Ferrell: Oh, for about three or four hours, and then we gave up. Uh, we had a home to go back to, and . . . uh . . . we had the shelter of our car . . . uh, but, uh . . . and you'd think we would have been able to. I'm not too proud of that, are you, Trev, that we couldn't do it? Uh, . . . the, the . . . the streets are cold, filthy, uh, how cold was it, Trevor, it was about thirty . . .

Trevor: Not that cold!

Ferrell: No, it was about thirty-eight degrees or something, and I thought, "well, that's not going to be so bad." Well, it *was* so bad, and we had sleeping bags with us, and we thought, uh, we'd be able to stand it. But, uh, the sidewalk's awfully hard, uh, you see raw sewage here and there, it's, it's not easy. And those people, uh, that spend their lives out there, uh, I don't know how they do it.

Neary: And yet you go down there frequently, all the time. At one point, I think you were going every night.

Ferrell: Yes, uh, the vans now, there, it's a big operation. The vans go in every night, uh, serving homeless people food—food that's, uh, generously donated by fast food chains, and, uh, there are volunteer . . . uh . . . coordinators of the effort, uh, individual families. There are over a hundred families in the Philadelphia area that cook on a regular basis, and food is . . . is . . . taken in and given freely, unconditionally to people that . . . that are on the streets and obviously have a need for, uh, for someone, so much more of a need for the . . . the caring that's exchanged than really the . . . the food, I guess.

Neary: What kind of reaction do you get from the street people when . . . when you go down there and . . . and start giving things away? 'N' it . . . was it different when you began? Has it changed over the course of time, or, do you get a variety of reactions?

Trevor: We get a lot of different reactions, a lot of them—they're all good, though. Like, they all accept the food, 'n' nice; some of them might not accept the food, but after a while, we'll wear them down, and they'll accept the food.

Neary: What do you mean "wear them down"?

Trevor: Like, they'll say no, but every night, we'd ask them, 'n' they'd say OK.

Ferrell: Yeah. Eventually, eventually, they say yeah, uh, and initially they, most of them say yes, uh, because it's a youngster that's offering it to them, and not someone towering over them and looking down on them, and saying "what are you doing out here, you ought to get a job?" Uh, kids are non—they're not judgmental, and uh, they're not threatening; they're just doing it, because of a heart-felt need to, want to reach out to somebody.

Neary: Trevor, this must have . . . this must have changed your life completely.

Trevor: Yeah, well I'm not allowed to . . . I'm not . . . I'm allowed, but I'm not able to play with my friends as much, and have as much fun as I used to. But it's all worth it: helping the homeless people on the streets, and seeing how grateful they are.

Neary: Mm-hm. Well, how has it changed you?

Trevor: Well, I know that . . . I've learned that people may look scary, but they're really nice, and to treat people not just because of what they look like or anything.

Neary: So you were scared when you first went down there.

Trevor: The first night, yes, but now I know there's nothing to be afraid of.

Neary: Trevor Ferrell and his father Frank Ferrell, who along with Trevor's mother

Janet, and with the help of Edward Waken, has written a book about his son's campaign for the homeless, called *Trevor's Place*. Proceeds from the book are being donated to Trevor's campaign.

UNIT 4: Where the Girls and Boys Are

Introduction: If you have been unlucky in love of late, listen carefully. Your problem may not be your personality, or even your breath. The problem may be statistical. This explanation from NPR's economics correspondent, Robert Krulwich.

Krulwich: According to the 1980 census, women and men are not spread evenly across the United States. There are regions where there is an abundance of men, and other places where there's an overload of women. And tonight, in case you're planning a move, we're going to tell you where the boys are, and where the girls are in this country. And since statistics are a little hard to do on the radio, we're gonna do this musically. Now remember, please, that with a few exceptions, there are generally more women than men in America; but for men looking for women, there are some states where, relatively speaking, men are now rare.

Singer: For every being of the male sex,
      Fish or fowl or Tyrannosaurus rex,
      For every being there should be a mate,
      But that's not so in every state.

Chorus: Where the girls are,
      Where there's more called "she" than there are called "he";
      Where the girls are,
      That's the place that we're longing to be.

Krulwich: All right, here are those places. States with elderly populations have more women. Since they, women, live longer, there are more of them around. Florida has 88½ men for every 100 women. Northeastern states with lots of clerical, finance, retail, insurance, banking, and health-care jobs—those jobs attract women, so the northeast, it turns out, pulls women out of the south and midwest. Therefore, for every 100 women, New Jersey has only 88 men; Pennsylvania, only 88 men; Rhode Island, only 86 men; New York State, only 85 men; and on the top of the list, the place in America where men statistically are most rare: the nation's capital, the District of Columbia: 82 men for every hundred women. The reason is that D.C. has a large black population and, according to the Census Bureau, the black and white races in America seem to have slightly different ratio boys and girls. Whites produce 106 boys for every hundred girls; blacks 103 boys for every hundred girls. So the blacks start out with fewer boys, plus black males die earlier than whites, which creates a preponderance of women in black communities like D.C., so that . . . where is where the women are. Now, how about . . . the men?

Singer: For every being of the female sex,
      Fish or fowl or Tyrannosaurus rex,
      For every being there should be a mate,
      But that's not so in every state.

Chorus: Where the boys are,
      Where there's more called "he" than there are called "she";
      Where the boys are,
      That's the place that we're longing to be.
                  (Chorus repeated)

Krulwich: Well, there're not many such places. Only four states have more men in them than women. For every hundred women, Nevada has 101 men; Wyoming, 104 men; Hawaii, 105 men; and at the very top of the list, with far more men than women, is the state of Alaska, 115.9 men for every hundred women. If that sounds heavy, during the gold rush eighty years ago in Alaska, according to the *Wall Street Journal*, for every hundred women, there were 259 men. The explanation is just the reverse of the northeast. The northeast has jobs that attract women from other regions. The western states have jobs in mining, agriculture, heavy industrial outdoor work which attracts men from all over. So as a general rule of thumb, and then we'll get back to the U.S. Census Chorus one more time, the west has the highest concentration of men; the south and the east, the highest concentration of women. So now you know.

Choruses *(combined men and women):*
> Where the boys/girls are,
> Where there's more called "he"/"she" than there are called "he"/"she,"
> Where the boys/girls are,
> That's the place that we're longing to be.
> > *(repeated)*

Krulwich: I'm Robert Krulwich reporting from New York.

Announcer: Thank you, Robert. By the way, our chorus featured Tracy Ula, Tamar Lewin, and Ira Flatow. Music by the Minnesota Scandinavian Ensemble, which has three men and one woman.

UNIT 5: The Thinking Cap

Introduction: In search of inspiration we may go for a walk, or stare out the window, or talk to friends. But Edward Brainard, of Marion, Massachusetts, has a different approach. He puts on a "thinking cap." Brainard has invented a cap that warms the brain, just by a degree or so. He says that makes the brain work better. Ed Brainard stumbled onto the idea quite by accident.

Brainard: Back in 19 ... 74, I had a two-year period when I had only one out of four children at home, the others were all off in school, and this one son, David, and I would sit in the ... uh ... kitchen ... uh ... at evening, waiting for supper to be cooked by our ... my wife, and one evening we just started talking on the subject of creativity. And at that instant, uh, David looked over at me across the dinner table and said, "Dad, uh, last time I had a fever ..." and at that instant, when he said "fever," he and I both said, "Why don't we heat the human head, and we will make people think faster, and maybe be more creative?" So finally I said, "I'm going to try it." I took two heating pads and came home one night and said to my wife and to David, "Here's tape, here's gauze, here's two heating pads. We're now going to form a thinking cap."

Chadwick: So you put together a couple of heating pads; you just taped them together and tried it out on yourself.

Brainard: Um, actually, it wasn't quite that easy. I put 'em together, and got the ... the basic controls to ... to work, and decided how high over the forehead I thought I should bring it down, and how low over the neck, and my wife ... uh ... would tape a little, and put the heating elements, and ... and I'd ... David and I would talk about it. It was being done over my head, and so we just kept adding the elements where I felt . . . uh . . . just fr . . . fr . . . with the feel of things, I felt, mentally, where they should go. And then that was the creation of the first heated helmet, which we call "The Thinking Cap."

Chadwick: When you first tried it out, could you right away uh . . . uh . . . see some result? Did you . . . did you think that you were doing, uh . . . more efficient or faster thinking?

Brainard: Um, I just had a feeling that something was uh . . . more positive, but the problem is, I was scared to do too much, and I wanted to move slowly, so I didn't hurt anybody. So, I then looked around for a way to prove that I really was doing something that was positive. My company . . . uh . . . funded a research uh . . . uh physiologist and psychologist out at University of Illinois in Urbana, and . . . uh . . . and he's been able to s . . . prove that, uh, all the work we did, and be able to show, when you do mathematical computations that you have a significant increase in speed—this may not sound like much—like 1 percent? Now think of this, if you were . . . uh . . . you have to think in terms of, like compounding money in a bank. If you were always 1 percent, doing 1 percent uh, better, than the other person compounding money, after ten years, you'd be way, way ahead. Now, the human being, if you were only 1 percent faster in computation, think of what after each eight-hour day where you might be done doing your job, how much further you might have traveled, in doing your tasks, or thinking out problems.

Chadwick: Edward Brainard invented "The Thinking Cap." He says he's in the process of marketing the cap now.

UNIT 6:   Who Is More Afraid of Nuclear War?

Introduction: A joint U.S.-Soviet opinion poll released today shows Russian teenagers fear a nuclear war far less than American teens. This is the first time Soviet authorities have allowed Americans to participate in administering a public opinion poll in the Soviet Union. Research psychologist Jonathon Tudge assisted in the project, and so did sociologist John Robinson.

Robinson: We interviewed a cross section of Maryland teenagers, students at, across the state of Maryland, 3,372, and . . . uh . . . this was seventh (through) twelfth grade, aged ten to seventeen.

Montaigne: And, Mr. Tudge, the Russian students?

Tudge: Yes, uh, just over 2,000 of them, in two regions of European Russia, the Tambov region and the Rostov-na-Donau region . . .

Montaigne: Mm-hm.

Tudge: . . . participated.

Montaigne: Now, fewer Russian students, as I understand it, thought nuclear war was likely, than did American students. Were they also optimistic that—should there be a nuclear war—that they, the Russian students, would survive it?

Robinson: No, the . . . uh . . . perceptions on that score were almost the same, that . . .

uh . . . about equal proportions thought that . . . uh . . . in majorities in both countries . . . uh . . . felt that they would not be able to survive a nuclear war.

Montaigne: And, retaliation, if we were attacked, or retaliation if they were attacked?

Robinson: In the Soviet Union . . . uh . . . 78 percent felt that if their country were attacked that they should retaliate, and . . . uh . . . the figure in the United States was 72 percent.

Montaigne: There was another question in the survey, and that was, I understand, the students were asked if they thought their children's lives would be better than their own lives.

Robinson: Yes, and we found almost three-quarters of Soviet students uh—again reflecting I think a more optimistic view—felt that life would be better for their children than for themselves. Uh . . . that was only true for about half of the . . . uh . . . Maryland students we interviewed.

Montaigne: Mr. Tudge, do you have any theories on why the Soviet youths appear to express more optimistic views about the future, about the nuclear arms race than do the American students?

Tudge: Russian children know an awful lot about what is likely to happen if there were to be a nuclear war. And, because they know so much about it, they feel it can't possibly happen. Over and over again, when you talk to Russian children, they answer this: things like, "Our leaders will never let it happen; it just couldn't happen." Also, in the Soviet Union, the mass media tends to focus primarily on the good side of life rather than disasters and so on.

Montaigne: Don't the Soviet viewers know that, to . . . to a large extent, there's editing going on there?

Tudge: Um . . . they are very little aware, I think, of the amount of editing that goes on. Yes, I . . . I tend to think that they, that the vast majority of them accept what they're told, without really thinking about it.

Montaigne: Mr. Robinson, you polled 3,400 students in just one state.

Robinson: Yes, that's correct.

Montaigne: Can that possibly be representative of a . . . of a very large nation—kids in Maryland, will they react the same way as kids in Nebraska, or California?

Robinson: Well, it looks like that's the case, because we used a number of questions that had been used on national surveys . . . uh . . . from the University of Michigan's uh . . . national study of monitoring the future, and we asked the same questions we . . . and we found that the answers that were given in Maryland were all within about two percentage points of what we found nationally.

Montaigne: Mm-hm. And, Mr. Tudge, the Soviets. Um, these particular provinces. What kind of places were they, and are they representative of the students . . . they're representative of the students in the rest of the Soviet Union?

Tudge: That's a little harder to answer. We were concerned not to have major centers like Moscow, Leningrad, Kiev—we wanted a more average sample—so we . . . we feel we have a . . . a pretty good representative sample of at least European Russia.

Montaigne: Jonathon Tudge is a research psychologist at the University of Utah. John Robinson is Director of the Survey Research Center at the University of Maryland.

UNIT 7: At the Table

Introduction: I'm Susan Stamberg. We begin with Craig Claiborne. He has been with us for several weeks now, offering ideas on summer eating. Now the food editor of the *New York Times* has something else on his mind: the manners we use at table. Craig Claiborne sees a decline in our manners.

Claiborne: Uh ... I'll tell you, Susan, it disturbs me a little bit. I would never go in public with ... with dirty fingernails. And I would not go out if I had my tie at half-mast, uh ... in uh ... proper ... company. Uh ... I wouldn't go out without brushing my teeth, and I think all these things are just the niceties of life. I like a casual life-style, and I lead a very casual life-style. I can laugh as hard as anybody else w ... about a good dirty joke. But, I think that when you are at table, there's so many nice things that can be done that uh ... uh ... are ignored by the masses of people when they do entertain. For example, you should never uh ... put a candle ... uh ... candles on a table that will impair the flow of vision.

Stamberg: Mm-hm.

Claiborne: Uh ... if you and I are sitting across from each other, the candles should be so low that you and I can look at each other—in each other's eyes—without being ... having our ... our vision marred by the candle flame.

Stamberg: And what about flowers? Same thing ...

Claiborne: The same thing is true. You should always have ... uh ... if you have flowers on the table, there should be an arrangement low enough so that ... uh ... you and I don't have to peek-a-boo, looking around the flower arrangement to see each other.

Stamberg: Mm.

Claiborne: Uh ... one of the uh ... the things that I uh ... also that I ... uh ... am a little bit nuts over on is wine service. Uh ... I see people setting a table, they'll take their fingers, and either put them inside of a glass in order to put 'em on the table, they'll put their fingers on the rim; I think this is not only unsightly, it's ... it's terribly unsanitary.

Stamberg: But it ... oh, it's so convenient, though. I'm guilty of this, I'm guil ...

Claiborne: No, you can hold the wine—a good wine glass always has a stem—and you can hold the wine glass by the stem, which you should, and you should never touch that rim with another part of your body except your lips.

Stamberg: Mm.

Claiborne: And it's also very fine, I think, to always wipe your lips before you ... before you ... take a sip of wine. There's nothing uh ... uh ...

Stamberg: What—each time?

Claiborne: Each time!

Stamberg: What, you just sit there, dabbing your lips—with a napkin, or you sleeve—

Claiborne: Well, oh, no, you don't ... oh, you don't have to be neurotic about it. But, uh ... lip stains around the rim of the glass, I think they're very unsightly things to see. Uh, there's one ... one thing that bothers me, uh ... and you hear it everywhere. Someone will come up and say, "Would you care for a glass of wine, or do you ca ...

like champagne?" That is the most annoying thing I can imagine. What do they think champagne is? Champagne is wine! So the proper way to . . . to phrase that, "Would you care for a glass of still wine, or would you care for a glass of champagne?"

Stamberg: Still wine or champagne? That's the distinction!

Claiborne: It's also important when you pour wine; you should always hold the wine bottle by the label, because if it . . . if you drip, if it's a red wine especially, if it drips down . . . uh . . . unless you've got that label held firmly in your . . . in your . . . uh . . . hand, the wine's going to drip down onto the label, and it's very, again, it's something very unsightly.

Stamberg: I thought you held it that way to cover up how cheap a bottle wine it was.

Claiborne: No, no. You should . . . you should always show the . . . show the wine to your guests . . . uh . . . before they start to drink.

Stamberg: Huh. But just peel off the price tag, that's what we do at our house. Craig Claiborne, thank you very much.

Claiborne: I thank you, Susan.

UNIT 8:   From One World to Another

Whiteman: *I'uni Kwi Athi? Hiatho.*
White horses, tails high, rise from the cedar.
Smoke brings the fat crickets,
trembling breeze.
Find that holy place, a promise.
Embers glow like moon air.

Stamberg: Roberta Hill Whiteman, reading from her first published collection of poetry, *Star Quilt.*

Whiteman: Will you brush my ear? An ice bear sometimes lumbers west.
Your life still gleams, the edge melting.
I never let you know.
You showed me how under snow and darkness,
grasses breathe for miles.

Stamberg: Roberta Hill Whiteman dedicated this poem to her father, using his Oneida Indian name for the title.

Whiteman: My father was Oneida and Mohawk. He raised us. My mother died when I was very young and . . . um . . . I never really thanked him. He died in the late sixties, when I was in my early twenties, and so, this poem, in a way, is trying to thank him for raising me.

Stamberg: Where did you grow up?

Whiteman: I grew up in Green Bay, Wisconsin, which is about ten miles from the Oneida reservation.

Stamberg: Not on the reservation itself.

Whiteman: No, I didn't grow up on the reservation. Uh . . . and a lot of times, we would go out there, but it's a very small reservation, and I did not grow up on it.

Stamberg: Mm-hm.

Whiteman: It's about eight by ten miles.

Stamberg: And do you feel, uh . . . uh . . . in going back, in . . . in going from Green Bay to Oneida, that you are moving from one world to another?

Whiteman: Oh yes! Oh, yes! I find there is quite a difference. When I go to Oneida . . . um . . . there's just this real feeling of uh . . . of everything being connected to each other, to the people, to the land, to the . . . the long-ago. That there is a sense of uh . . . of community, and I never really felt that as a child. Um . . . as a child, I often felt that I was somehow exiled . . . uh . . . that I ended up in this very large place, and that . . . that I didn't quite understand or I didn't feel connected to the other people around me.

Stamberg: Mm-hm.

Whiteman: And I think in . . . in one way that's why I turned to poetry. It made me feel connected to things.

Stamberg: Hah; hah. Because I wanted to ask you, what influences your poetry most, do you think? The fact that you are Indian, or the fact that you are a woman, or the fact that you are a wife, or a mother, or a daughter? Because you write about all of those things.

Whiteman: Well, I think, as a child, my grandmother was a Mohawk, and she used to tell us a . . . lots of stories, and she loved poetry, and as a child, some of the books that we had were her books of poetry, and I often spent a lot of time . . . uh . . . poring over her books, or listening to her talk. And I think I found in language . . . um . . . pictures in my mind that made me feel really happy, or helped me to deal with things. And um . . . I don't think it's any one particular part of my uh . . . social being, mother, or . . . or whatever, my . . . my heritage, but I think it is that that voice that my grandmother made me pay attention to.

Overcast Dawn

This morning I feel dreams dying.
One trace is this feather
fallen from a gull,
with its broken shaft,
slight white down,
and long dark tip
that won't hold air.
How will you reach me
if all our dreams are dead?

Stamberg: You write a lot about natural things, and . . . and deal with nature in . . . in ways that I've not come across before. I wonder if that's where . . . um . . . maybe that Indian heritage really . . . uh . . . shows through, just being able to look at a feather that way.

Whiteman: My father . . . uh . . . tried to get me to listen and to pay attention; and . . . uh . . . I guess that's where part of that comes from.

Stamberg: Roberta Hill Whiteman, her first collection of poetry is called *Star Quilt*. It's published by the Holy Cow Press in Minneapolis. It has a foreword by the poet Carolyn Forché.

UNIT 9:   To Finish First

Introduction: Dogs coming straight down the chute. Rick Mackie comes across. The winner of the 1983 Iditarod Sled Dog Race.

Adams: Susan, is there a way that you can tell that . . . uh . . . the dogs are disappointed that . . . uh . . . you all didn't win?

Susan: Well, they definitely are. They know the difference. And, they're eager to pass anybody that they can. We passed . . . um . . . something like seven teams the last day of the race, so they were very pleased about that. But they can feel the difference in me upon coming across the finish line.

Adams: Susan Butcher crossed the finish line of the 1983 Iditarod Trail Sled Dog Race last Friday, one day behind the winner, Rick Mackie. Out of sixty-eight entrants, she came in ninth. The Iditarod is an eleven-hundred-mile or so two-week run through Alaska from Anchorage up to Nome. Susan Butcher finished second last year, and we talked with her the day before she started out on this year's Iditarod, and today Susan Butcher still has a cold she caught at the beginning of that race, otherwise she's recovered pretty well.

Susan: I fell well rested. I think almost you learn; your body learns that it's gonna put up with two weeks of this abuse every year, and . . . uh . . . tolerates it beta—I tolerate it better and better every year.

Adams: Yeah. You finished ninth. Is that, a . . . just a tremendous disappointment for you?

Susan: Well, yes, it is, for a number of reasons. Um . . . the first ten days of the race, I was um . . . my team was by far and away . . . um . . . one of the very best in the team, and I was situated in the best position. Um . . . the team was doing well, they were getting tons of rest, until getting to Grayling . . . uh . . . they had had a local race there, called the Yukon 200, a two-hundred-mile race, about a month prior to the Iditarod. And they had marked the trail with the same type of markings the Iditarod uses.

Adams: Oh.

Susan: And, they had failed to mark the Iditarod trail. And so I headed up the Yukon 200. And was lost for eight hours, and uh . . . the dog team just . . . uh . . . got real confused and they just lost a lot of their confidence.

Adams: Since we talked to you last, we've had some letters, people asking about your dogs. And . . . uh . . . I wanted to ask, did you have to leave any dogs along the way this time?

Susan: Yeah, I did. I started with fourteen, and I had to leave four of them, um, at different places.

Adams: You don't just abandon them?

Susan: No, they're already back here with me. They get flown either up to Nome, or back to Anchorage.

Adams: And there're veterinarians along the way?

Susan: There're veterinarians at almost every checkpoint. In addition to being out there to help you, they're also out there in case, because of fatigue, and other things, the musher's decision-making process is not as good as it is in Anchorage, and they will say, "hey, this dog doesn't look all that good, maybe you ought to drop him, you know."

Adams: The . . . uh . . . the amount of money you won, $3,200, is that enough to . . . to uh . . . support your training for next year's Iditarod? The whole year?

Susan: My training costs about $40,000 a year.

Adams: Goodness.

Susan: So, no. *(laughs)* The answer to that is a definite no.

Adams: Tell us about . . . uh . . . the finish of the race this year. You came in a day after, almost a whole day after the leader. Uh, that last push toward the finish line, for you, what was it like—how . . . how much sleep did you miss during that period of time, for example?

Susan: Well, you get about an hour of sleep a day; for the last three-hundred miles, from Unalakleet on, once you hit the coast, it's pretty much a constant push for the musher. Um, you're resting the dogs, say, you're mushing them five to six hours, and then resting them four. But a four-hour rest provides no rest for the mushers, 'cause we have to cook for them, and feed them.

Adams: And, when you crossed the line, did you, um, have any thoughts about next year? Did you say—I would say, of course—never again, never again will I . . .

Susan: *(laughs)* Well, I don't know. I did think of taking a year off, when I had some trouble out there and stuff, I was fairly . . . uh . . . disgusted with the . . . uh . . . marking of the trail, and that just because of that, you know, my . . . uh . . . all my hard work for the winter could go down the drain. But, shortly after coming in, and with everybody's well-wishes, and hoping that I'll win it again next year, uh . . . it's . . . easy to get right back into the swing of it. So it looks like I'll be running again.

Adams: Susan Butcher, talking with us from Anchorage. By the way, twenty teams are still out on the trail. The Iditarod was started ten years ago, to help commemorate a heroic relay of sled dog drivers in 1925, bringing life-saving serum to Nome to stave off a diphtheria epidemic.

UNIT 10:   Meet You on the Air

Susan Block: It's not just another Saturday night. It is Susan Block's "Date Night," and I'm Susan Block!

Kaufman: A call-in show for singles. Every Saturday night, on Los Angeles radio station KIEV. People meet on the air; they chat, and if they want, they write to each other's box number. Susan Block plays matchmaker.

Susan: Let's get personal with John. Hi there, John.

John: Yeah, hello, how are you?

Susan: I'm just fine, how are you?

John: Oh, fine. I had a wonderful night tonight, I had guests over, played the piano, had a lot of fun, oh, great.

Susan: I hear the piano.

John: Oh, yeah, it's me. *(sings)*
More than the greatest love the world has known
This is the love I'll give to Linda alone

Susan: Linda! Linda, where are you? C.J., get Linda on the line. She'll have to . . . she'll have to hear how she's being serenaded to . . .

John: Serenaded, yeah!

Susan: OK, Linda?

Linda: Yes?

Susan: How did you like that serenade?

Linda: Oh, that was very nice.

Susan: Well, here's John; he'd like to talk to you.

Linda: OK.

John: Hi, Linda!

Linda: Hi. What do you like to do?

John: I like to discover new things, invent new ideas, uh . . . go to the beach . . . uh . . . enjoy . . .

Kaufman: The show's host is a self-confessed personal-ad voyeur. She wrote a book on how to play the personals, and promoted it on the talk-show circuit.

Susan: And sometimes what I'd do with a call-in show is, somebody would call in, and—say it was Linda—and I would make up a personal for Linda. And she would express herself and then get off the air. And then maybe Bob would call in and say "Hey, that Linda, she sounded great, how can I meet her?" And I would just feel terrible that I couldn't match up poor Bob and poor Linda, who were two single people who needed each other. And I thought, "I'm gonna do a show like this myself. I'm gonna match people up on the air," and that's how "Date Night" started.

Kaufman: The banter is that of a singles bar. What kind of work do you do? What movies have you seen? And, do you like Chinese food?

Female voice: What are your favorites?

Male Voice: Sizzling chicken, and hot and sour soup, and all kinds of great stuff.

Female Voice: All right . . .

Susan: I'll bet there are some other sizzling things you can think of to do.

Male Voice: Oh, yes, yes . . .

Female Voice: As long as we can pick and choose, and share plates, and . . .

Male Voice: Definitely.

Female Voice: There are a lot of other things too.

Male Voice: But you gotta use chop sticks.

Female Voice: Oh, I do all the time!

Male Voice: Good.

Kaufman: One of the things you do on the show is you have personal ads.

Susan: Yes. These are little messages that people make up. They can be anywhere from fifteen seconds to a minute long, and they're like the personals in the paper, except they're audio version. And . . . uh . . . you not only get information about people, you get a sense of their personality through their voice, and the best ones have music in the background to enhance the personality. Now, here's Robert, number 603.

Robert: Hi. I'm Robert, and I'm forty-three years old, six feet tall, 165 pounds, and I'm in excellent L.A. condition. I'm a passionate eccentric, and I am definitely an acquired taste. Some women have found me very beautiful.

Susan: I don't like the bland ads that I see in the paper. I don't like when everybody sounds like another single white female . . . uh . . . you know, professional, attractive, articulate, walks on the beach, sensuous, you know, blah, blah, blah, and so on and so forth, you know what I mean? I mean, it's all the same. Now, when people call in to put ads on my show, I tell them, "Look, I want you to be yourself, I mean, the part of you that is different." I don't care how bland a person they may seem to be on the outside, they'll sound outrageous on a personal.

Female Voice: I'm thirty-seven, and I look OK, I don't believe I've ever embarrassed anybody I went out with. I'm lookin' for somebody who's . . . uh . . . lookin' for somebody, I guess. I guess that says it: just a-lookin' for somebody that's lookin' for somebody. And my name's Annie. That's all.

Susan: That is as personal as we can get tonight, folks. This is Susan Block's "Date Night." Tune in next week; same time, same station, for another Saturday night on "Date Night."

UNIT 11: There Are Worse Things than Dying

Jason: My name is Jason Gaes. I live at 1109 Omaha Avenue in Worthington, Minnesota. I am eight years old and I have cancer.

Montaigne: Jason is now nine years old. He's written a book. It's been printed in his own handwriting, titled *My book for kids with cansur*. Adults provided the subtitle, *A Child's Autobiography of Hope*. In the book, Jason describes how he was treated for cancer diagnosed when he was six years old with a rare and fast-spreading form of cancer called Burkitt's lymphoma.

Jason: Radiation is really easy. All you have to do is lay there, and they put straps around your head so you don't move. And then it's over, and you come back tomorrow. But don't wash the Xs off of your head until they're done.

Montaigne: Jason, that's page three of the book, and there's a picture here, of, I guess it's you . . .

Jason: Yeah.

Montaigne: . . . lying on a table . . .

Jason: Mm-hm.

Montaigne: . . . and the word "radiation." Who drew the picture?

Jason: My two brothers, Adam and Tim. They're better than me, so I let them draw the pictures.

Montaigne: But you wrote the whole book.

Jason: Yeah.

Montaigne: There are books out, for kids, with cancer. You must have seen them, when you first found out you had cancer?

Jason: One time I came home with a . . . a book, and it was called *Hang Tough*, and I thought it was really neat, because that boy was going through the same . . . same things as I was going through, and the last two or three pages it told about . . . he died, and . . . and it stunk.

Montaigne: It stunk?

Jason: Uh-huh.

Montaigne: 'Cause he died?

Jason: Uh-huh. I didn't plan for that boy to die because he wrote such a nice book and all. When I wrote this book, I . . . uh . . . I kinda insteada tellin' about Jason Gaes died . . . uh . . . said that Jason Gaes lived.

Montaigne: In one page you write that having cancer isn't fun.

Jason: It ain't no party.

Montaigne: But you . . . you point out a couple of fun things.

Jason: Uh . . . I get lotsa nice presents, 'n' your Mom almost does anything you want her to do.

Montaigne: You also write about the different things that a kid would have to go through.

Jason: Mm-hm.

Montaigne: What were the parts that weren't so easy?

Jason: The bone marrow and the spinals, and the leg pains are probably the worst of it all. I had to have lots of help for the . . . for the bone marrow, because . . . I was almost purple, 'cause it hurt so much.

Montaigne: And the spinal tap. You have a picture here of a little boy, curled up tight.

Jason: Mm-hm. If you do that, it goes a lot faster.

Montaigne: Mrs. Gaes, Jason, in his book, writes about some bad moments.

Mrs. Gaes: Mm-hm.

Montaigne: How did he hold up?

Mrs. Gaes: For the most part, very, very well. Jason . . . uh . . . insisted on not being treated as a sick child. There were times when he needed me and I needed him, when, you know, like right in the middle of a spinal. But otherwise he came right out of the room and . . . went back to his normal activities.

Montaigne: Jason, you wrote this book because you said you were tired of reading books about kids who had cancer and who died in the end. Was there any time, during all this treatment, when you thought maybe dying wouldn't be so bad?

Jason: When it was all over with, 'cause I thought I like, I would die if, um, right in the middle of a bone marrow.

Mrs. Gaes: About six months into treatment, Jason had had a lot of very aggressive treatment that left him very weak and very sick. And sometimes on the way up to Rochester, we'd stop on the Interstate and Jason would become so apprehensive that he would start to vomit before we got there. And I stopped, on the Interstate, to help him— he was sick to his stomach—and he just looked at me and said, "Mom, I don't want to do this anymore." And I told him, "Well, you . . . you know what will happen, Jason, if we don't do this." And he told me, "Yeah, but there are worse things than dyin'." And when I read his book, I was stunned, because I . . . I guess I didn't realize how well he had dealt with the possibility of death and dying. If you read his book, you'll see that he compares death to coming out of my womb. He says "When I was a baby in my mom's stomach, I didn't want to come out. The doctor had to give my mom a shot, to make me come out. But now that I'm outside, I would never want to go back in my mom's stomach." And he said, "I think going to heaven is like that. Once we get there, we won't want to come back here." So he had no paralyzing fear of dying. It was the treatment, the pain that they would inflict upon him that he was afraid of.

Jason: If you get scared, and can't quit, go and talk to your Mom, and she can rock you, or rub your hair. Or if you want, you can call me. My number is 507–376–3824. And when you feel real bad, it's OK to cry.

Montaigne: Jason, have kids called you?

Jason: Yeah, you bet! Lots of kids have called me. One little girl was gonna have . . . well, she's about my age, she'd be seven right now, and she asked me, um, what she should do, 'cause she was gonna have a treatment the day after she called me, and I kinda told her that you can't feel anything after the . . . thing is done. You'll feel a little dry, and sick to your stomach, but to me there was really nothin' wrong with the operation.

Montaigne: Has anyone called you back to tell you that it helped to talk to you before they had something done?

Jason: Yeah, this, matter of fact, the same little girl. She said that it really worked.

Montaigne: Jason Gaes, along with his mother Sissy. Jason is the author of *My book for kids with cansur.* Doctors have now told Jason that his cancer is completely cured, and that there's no chance for a relapse.

Jason: And the rest of the days, when you don't have treatments, try to forget you have cancer and think about something else. Shoot baskets, or go swimming.

UNIT 12:   A Couch Potato

Introduction: Robert Armstrong, a cartoonist and illustrator in Dixon, California, claims to have coined the phrase "couch potato" back in 1976. The phrase just doesn't seem that old, although the tradition of lounging on a couch, surrounded by junk food and fizzy drinks, eyes fixed on the TV set, that tradition is certainly time honored. In addition to the phrase, Mr. Armstrong is founder and head of Couch Potato Clubs around the country. There are 8,500 members, he says. They get an official Couch Potato handbook, plus newsletters and the obligatory T-shirt. Robert Armstrong says this is an important weekend for Couch Potatoes.

Armstrong: The holidays are always important; it's a family time; everyone watches the football games; at least the men folk are in there watching the football game, and the women are in some other room, maybe the kitchen, 'er talking about family matters, or other matters, and . . . uh . . . in some respects, it's one way for all these different people in the family to get . . . they . . . to get together in one room and tolerate one another, around the video hearth, that is, watching TV.

Stamberg: So it helps keep the peace over a long family weekend, huh?

Armstrong: Yeah, if they have nothing else in common, they can all watch the same TV program. And there's a definite need for a group like the Couch Potatoes, I think.

Stamberg: What do you think the need is?

Armstrong: I think firstly, there are a lot of people that suffer from intellectual guilt about how much TV they watch, and . . . uh . . . for years it's been everyone's little dirty secret about TV watching—and how much they watched—and people would lie about it, and we as Couch Potatoes beckon people to "come out of the closet," and claim it loud that they are a "tuber and proud." The "tuber" part of it is one of the reasons why we selected the potato to be our icon, because it is, after all, a tuber, and has many eyes.

Stamberg: Oh, I just got it—as in tube!

Armstrong: Yes, watching the tube, and all the eyes of the potato used to watch TV with. It just, seemed like a . . . a good symbol for us to rally around. And . . . uh . . . though, I think many outsiders have . . . uh . . . teased us about our physiques taking on a sort of a potato shape after awhile, but . . . uh . . . that's not necessarily bad; have a potato shape, it gives you the needed ballast so you don't roll off the couch quite so readily.

Stamberg: *(laughing)* What's usually highest on the Couch Potatoes' hit parade of TV shows—would it be "Love Boat"?

Armstrong: That's just one that came to mind, but we have so many members, from such a wide cross-section of walks of life, that . . . uh . . . I'd have to say that any show would be a recommended Couch Potato show. In fact, we have a slogan we live by, "If it's on TV, it must be good."

Stamberg: Words to live by, for all you Couch Potatoes out there. Robert Armstrong in Dixon, California. A man of very discriminating taste, obviously. He is the founder and head of Couch Potato Clubs around the nation, a position, I'm sure, cheers his mother.

ACKNOWLEDGMENTS

Many people contributed to the development of this book, both in the ideas for its content and in the refinement of individual activities.

I am especially grateful to my two editors at Longman, Joanne Dresner and Penny Laporte. Joanne's vision and continual support for my work have helped me complete a second project. Penny's insights and direction during the editing process helped me reshape the book to better meet our objectives. It has been a wonderful experience working with both of them.

This second book could never have been possible without the help of my colleagues at The American Language Program, Columbia University. I would like to thank the chairman, Mary Jerome, who has offered me continual support in my academic pursuits. I would also like to thank Frances Boyd, Karen Brockmann, Winnie Falcon, Sally Fairman, Gail Hammer, Sheri Handel, Jane Kenefick, David Mumford, Polly Merdinger, Barbara Miller, David Quinn, Helene Rubenstein, Shelley Saltzman, Janice Sartori, Linda Schlam, Bill Schweers, Jane Sturtevant, Joanne Warren, and Brian Young. Their willingness to try out the materials with their students and provide comments and suggestions for revisions was invaluable. In addition, I would like to give special thanks to Gail Fingado for being an invaluable resource for the grammar exercises in this book and Dick Faust and Shelley Saltzman for contributing pun exercises.

I would also like to thank Carole Rosen and Elly Kellman at the English Language Institute, Hunter College, for their feedback on specific units. And special thanks goes to my friend and colleague, Peter Thomas, for organizing the piloting of the material at Hunter College.

Sherry Preiss, of Language Training Institute, was once again an important contributor to this project. Sherry piloted the book with her students, and many of her suggestions have been incorporated into this book. I thank her for her time and insights.

Once again, I am indebted to the staff at National Public Radio. They have been most supportive in my completing yet another project. Their willingness to see the project through the various stages of development has shown me that they are true educators, as they believe in extending the use of their programming to classroom settings. I am especially grateful to Carolyn Gershfeld, who was the first person to recognize the value of writing a book for intermediate-level students. Because of her enthusiasm for my work, this second project could be realized. I would also like to thank Joanne Wallace for her willingness to take responsibility for the project halfway through its completion. Theodora Brown was extremely helpful in facilitating some of the more difficult legal processes. I thank her for her support and for her warmth. Wendy Blair did a superb job in producing the accompanying cassettes. Finally, I owe many thanks to the librarians at National Public Radio: Jaclin Gilbert, Beth Howard, Sara Levy, Margot McGann, and Lisa Reginbald. They were very helpful in directing me to the level of materials needed for this book and in providing me with ideas for the content of various units.

And finally, I would like to thank my husband, Eric. Without his continual encouragement and belief in my ability to write, a second book would never have been possible.

CREDITS

We wish to thank the following for providing us with photographs or artwork:

Page 1, courtesy of General Foods USA;

Page 9, National Center for Health Statistics;

Page 20, Deborah Robinson, 1989;

Page 35, Career Blazers *(top)* and U.S. Department of Labor *(bottom)*;

Page 46, Philadelphia Convention and Visitors Bureau;

Page 55, U.S. Air Force;

Pages 66 and 94, David Brownell, © State of New Hampshire, 1986;

Page 75 (Jennifer Hill, Oneida tribal member), photo by Keith Skenandore;

Page 86, photo by Jim Brown;

Page 105, Tim and Adam Gaes, from *My book for kids with cansur*, copyright 1987 by Jason Gaes, reproduced by permission, Melius & Peterson Publishing, Inc. (for more information, call 1–800–882–5171);

Pages 118 and 123, Robert Armstrong.